Everyday Grammar and Usage

SIMPLIFIED AND SELF-TAUGHT

SHARON SORENSON

Chairman, English Department
Central High School
Evansville, Indiana

AN ARCO BOOK
Published by Prentice Hall Press
New York, NY 10023

DEDICATION

This book is dedicated to my students, who suggested that I write it.

ACKNOWLEDGMENTS

My special thanks to Selma Bubenzer, a devoted scholar and special friend, for her editorial comments and suggestions.

My sincere thanks to Virginia Thrasher for her encouragement and advice.

First Edition

Copyright © 1982 by Arco Publishing, Inc.
All rights reserved
including the right of reproduction
in whole or in part in any form

An Arco Book
Published by Prentice Hall Press
A Division of Simon & Schuster, Inc.
Gulf + Western Building
One Gulf + Western Plaza
New York, NY 10023

PRENTICE HALL PRESS is a trademark of Simon & Schuster, Inc.

Manufactured in the United States of America

4 5 6 7 8 9 10

Library of Congress Cataloging in Publication Data

Sorenson, Sharon.
   Everyday grammar and usage, simplified and self-taught.

   1. English language—Grammar—1950–   2. English language—Self-
instruction.   3. English language—Usage.
I. Title.
PE1112.S67   428.2   82-1683
ISBN 0-668-05434-4   AACR2

TABLE OF CONTENTS

Table of Contents

Table of Contents

INTRODUCTION

To the Reader:

So you never were sure whether to say "between you and I" or "between you and me"? And you never could understand how to use the two verbs *lie* and *lay* correctly? And no one could ever explain to you the difference between *who* and *whom* in a way that you could understand? And you know your punctuation is terrible. Commas drop in and out of your sentences at a whim. But you never could understand all that grammar stuff. Well, grammar does not have to be impossible or even confusing. This book is designed to help you find your way through standard grammar and usage problems with simple, easy-to-see solutions. Although this book does not handle grammar in the usual way and will not make a grammarian of you, you will no doubt find that the hints and tricks included will help you cope with whatever more traditional approaches you may confront. Because the aim of this book is to be practical, you will find rules and terminology at a minimum and emphasis placed on standard usage. And, after all, most people study grammar in an effort to achieve standard usage.

So, here it is: a practical, nongrammarian's grammar and handbook.

This book will deal with five parts of speech:

nouns

verbs

adjectives

adverbs

prepositions

For each of the five parts of speech, we will consider:

definition

function

characteristics

Most of what makes a word important in grammar is how it *functions*. Recognize from the beginning, however, that many words can function in more than one way; how a word functions determines what part of speech it is in that particular instance.

I

FUNDAMENTALS

1

CLASSIFICATION OF WORDS

PART I: NOUNS

A. **Definition:** A noun is the name of a person, place, or thing. (That is a traditional definition, but sometimes it is inadequate!)

Example:
Singing in the *shower* is not for *me*.
(*Singing* is the name of a thing; *shower* is the name of a place; and *me* is the substitute-name of a person.)

Often, definition alone is not sufficient to determine part of speech accurately. For instance, you may have looked at *singing* in the sentence above and thought at first that it looked like a verb. Without considering *function*, you may not recognize all nouns.

B. **Function:** A noun most commonly functions in one of three ways:

1. As the subject of a verb

   Example:
   Some *elephants* dance.
   (*Elephants,* a noun, is subject of the verb *dance.*)

2. As an object

   a. As direct object of the verb

      Example:
      One elephant danced a *jig*.
      (*Jig*, a noun, is the direct object of the verb *danced.*)

   b. As an indirect object of the verb

      Example:
      The trainer gave the *elephant* an apple.
      (*Elephant*, a noun, is now the indirect object of the verb *gave.*)

   c. As object of the preposition

      Example:
      The elephant danced another jig for the *trainer*.
      (*Trainer*, a noun, is the object of the preposition *for.*)

d.   As object of a verbal

Example:
The elephant liked dancing *jigs.*
(Jigs, a noun, is the object of *dancing.)*

3.   As a predicate word

Example:
The elephant is a *dancer.*
(Dancer, a noun, is the predicate noun after the linking verb *is.)*

Perhaps you are saying by now that you do not understand enough about such things as *direct objects* and *objects of verbals* (topics discussed in later chapters) for function to help you determine parts of speech. Later, however, when you have studied Chapter 2, you may come back and review function for additional clarity. These two chapters work hand-in-hand.

For now, though, however limited your understanding may be at this point concerning function, you will want also to consider noun *characteristics.*

C.   **Characteristics:**   A noun may have the following characteristics that will help you distinguish it from other parts of speech. Not all nouns will have every one of the following characteristics.

1.   Certain endings indicate nouns:

a.   Nouns can be made plural, usually by adding *-s* or *-es.*

Examples:
elephant, elephant*s;* trainer, trainer*s;* circus, circu*ses*

Note:
Some nouns have peculiar plural forms, like *child, children; goose, geese,* but most nouns can be made plural.

b.   Nouns can be made possessive by adding either an apostrophe and *-s* or an apostrophe only. When the noun is possessive, it functions as an *adjective.*

Examples:
tree, tree*'s* leaves, leaves, leave*s'* colors

2.   Certain words often appear in front of nouns:

a.   Articles: *a, an,* and *the*

Examples:
the tree, *a* tree, *an* earring, *a* ruby earring

Note:
For every article appearing in a sentence, there will be a noun following, although that noun may not be the very next word.

b.   Adjectives (words that describe shape, size, appearance, or number)

Examples:
tall, cone-shaped tree (describes size and shape of tree)
three golden maple trees (describes number, kind and appearance of trees)

In other words, certain characteristics will serve as a test to determine whether or not a word is a noun. If that word can be made plural (you can count them), or if that word can show ownership, or if that word can have *a, an,* or *the* in front, you can bet it will be a noun.

Look at the following nonsense sentence:

> When the jibjam quots the glitstat after a purdletroe warkled the clatter-strow, the barmel praesslebrow was strottled by an ubby warkened.

Certain words in the sentence above are obviously nouns. Can you recognize them? Consider characteristics. Find all the articles (*a, an,* and *the*). You know that a noun has to follow an article, although maybe not immediately. (There may be an adjective or two between the article and the noun.) If you still do not know whether or not a word is a noun, check for plural forms. Then consider *function.* When you think you have found all the nouns, check your answers with those below.

Nouns in the nonsense sentence:

> *jibjam* (*The* appears in front, and it is the subject of the verb *quots.*)
>
> *flitstat* (*The* appears in front, and it is the direct object of the verb *quots.*)
>
> *purdletroe* (*A* appears in front, and it is the subject of the verb *warkled.*)
>
> *clatterstrow* (It is the direct object of *warkled.*)
>
> *praesslebrow* (*The,* as well as the adjective *barmel,* appears in front, and it is the subject of the verb *strottled.*)
>
> *warkened* (*An,* as well as the adjective *ubby,* appears in front, and it is the object of the preposition *by.*)

PART II: VERBS

A. **Definition:** A verb shows action or state of being. This definition itself indicates that there are two kinds of verbs. As a result, there are also two basic functions:

B. **Function:**

1. Some verbs show action.

   Example:
   Some students *chatter* constantly.
   (*Chatter* shows an action that the students are doing.)

2. Some verbs link the subject to the predicate word.

   Example 1:
   Some students *are* noisy.
   (*Are* is a state of being or linking verb and links *students* to *noisy.*
   Noisy describes *students. Noisy* is a predicate adjective.)

   Example 2:
   These young men and women *are* students.

(*Are* now links *men* and *women* with *students. Students* renames *men* and *women. Students* is a predicate noun.)

Because verbs and verbals look so much alike, sometimes it is difficult to determine part of speech when one knows only definition and function. *Characteristics* will help you separate verbs from verbals.

C. **Characteristics:** Verbs show the following characteristics:

1. A verb changes time (or *tense*).
   To test for a verb, insert the words *yesterday* or *tomorrow* in front of the sentence. The word that changes is the verb.

   Example:
   They were singing in three-part harmony.
   Yesterday, they were singing in three-part harmony. (no change)
   Yesterday, they sang in three-part harmony.
   Tomorrow, they will sing in three-part harmony.

   From this simple test, you know that the word that changed, *were singing,* is the verb.

   Note:
   You will often need to try *both yesterday* and *tomorrow* if you do not know in which time (or tense) the sentence is written.

   a. Because a verb changes time, it has certain endings: *-s, -ed, -en, -ing.*

      Examples:
      The bear *ambles* along the path.
      The bear *ambled* along the path.
      The bear *will amble* along the path.
      The bear *is ambling* along the path.

      Hint:
      Do not confuse the -s *ending on the verb with the* -s *ending on nouns. We add an* -s *to nouns to make them* plural; *we add an* -s *to verbs to make them* singular.

      Examples:
      The bears (plural *noun*) amble (plural *verb*).
      The bear (singular *noun*) ambles (singular *verb*).

   b. Because a verb changes time, it also may have certain helping verbs (or *auxiliaries*):

do	have	could	may	will
does	has	would	might	shall
did	had	should	must	
	is	was	be	
	am	were	been	
	are		being	

Note:
The helper plus the main verb equals the complete verb phrase:
helper(s) + main verb = complete verb phrase

could
+
have } + *spanked* = could have been spanked
+
been

Some of the helping verbs can be used alone as main verbs; but when they appear with other verbs after them, they are helpers.

Example 1:
Marty and Jo *have* their homework.
(*Have* is the entire verb.)

Example 2:
Marty and Jo *should have* their homework.
(*Should* is a helper for the main verb *have*.)

Example 3:
Marty and Jo *have finished* their homework.
(*Have* is a helper for the main verb *finished; finished* appears after *have*.)

Example 4:
Gerry *should have finished* her homework.
(*Should* and *have* are both helpers; *finished* appears after *have* and *should* and therefore is the main verb.)

Note:
The verb that appears *last* in the verb phrase is the main verb.

So, the first characteristic of a verb is that it changes time. Now you are ready for the second and third characteristics:

2. Most verbs show action.

   a. The subject does something. (The verb is in active voice.)

   Example:
   That boy *ate* a grasshopper!

   b. The subject has something done to it.
   (The verb is in passive voice.)

   Example:
   The grasshopper *was eaten* by that boy.

3. Some verbs are linking. There are two kinds of linking verbs:

   a. Verbs that are always linking verbs:

is	*was*	*be*
am	*were*	*been*
are		*being*

Note:
These verbs are always linking when they are the *main* verbs. If they are merely *helping* verbs, they are *not* linking.

Example 1:
She *could have been* a beautiful girl.
(*Been* is the main verb, so the verb is linking.)

Example 2:
Linda *is being treated* for a serious illness.
(*Is* and *being* are only helpers for the main verb *treated,* so the verb is action, not linking.)

b. Verbs that can be linking verbs or action verbs:

seem	*appear*	*remain*
become	*grow*	*stay*

look	
smell	
taste	verbs of the senses
sound	
feel	

The trick of it, of course, is to be able to recognize when these verbs are action verbs and when they are linking verbs.

To Check:
Substitute some form of *to be* (*is, am, are, was, were, be, been,* or *being*) for any one of these eleven verbs. If the substitution makes sense, that verb is linking.

Example 1:
He *felt* miserable.
He *was* miserable.
(A form of *to be* works, so *felt* is a linking verb.)

Example 2:
She *felt* the fabric.
She *was* the fabric.
(No! *Felt* in this sentence is *not* a linking verb.)

Example 3:
He *tasted* the cake.
He *was* the cake.
(No! *Tasted* here is *not* a linking verb.)

Example 4:
The cake *tasted* delicious.
The cake *was* delicious.
(A form of *to be* works, so *tasted* is a linking verb.)

Warning:
Be aware that a form of *to be* can substitute for other verbs that will *not* be linking:

Example:
The pictures *hung* on the wall.
The pictures *were* on the wall.

But *hung* is *not* a linking verb. It is not one of the eleven verbs listed in (b) above.

When words like *hung* appear in a sentence, you may wish to check your dictionary to see whether or not the verb can function as a linking verb.

Sometimes, it is difficult to know whether the verb is a linking verb followed by a predicate word or if the verb is, in fact, a verb phrase.

Examples:
The author was dedicated to his work.

The book was dedicated to the author's students.

The author is dedicating the book to her students.

In the first sentence, *was* is the linking verb, and *dedicated* is a predicate adjective. In the second sentence, the verb is *was dedicated*. In the third sentence, the verb is *is dedicating*. How can you tell? Where there is some form of *to be* (*is, am, are, was, were, be, been,* or *being*) plus another word that looks like a verb, insert the word *very* after the verb *to be.* If *very* makes sense, the verb is a linking verb with a predicate word. If *very* does *not* make sense, then you have a verb phrase.

Example 1:
The author was [very] dedicated to his work.
(Because *very* works here, you know that *was* is a linking verb.)

Example 2:
The book was [very] dedicated to the author's students.
(Because *very* does not make sense, you know the verb phrase is *was dedicated.*)

Example 3:
The author is [very] dedicating the book to her students.
(*Very* does not work; the verb phrase is *is dedicating.*)

PART III: ADJECTIVES

A. **Definition:** An adjective describes or modifies a noun.

B. **Function:** An adjective will answer one of these questions about a noun:

1. *Which one?*

Example:
The *broken* chair was in the *south* hall.
(*Broken* describes which *chair,* and *south* tells which *hall.*)

2. *What kind?*

    Example:
    Her *wool* sweater kept out the *biting* cold.
    (*Wool* describes what kind of sweater, and *biting* describes what kind of *cold.*)

3. *How many?*

    Example:
    Seven students attended the meeting.
    (*Seven* tells how many *students.*)

4. *Whose?*

    Example:
    The *student's* chair was outside *her* door.
    (*Student's* describes whose *chair,* and *her* describes whose *door.*)

Remember that one of the characteristics of a noun is that adjectives can appear in front of it. This means that each of the words being described above is a noun:

the *broken* (adjective) *chair* (noun)

the *south* (adjective) *hall* (noun)

the *wool* (adjective) *sweater* (noun)

the *biting* (adjective) *cold* (noun)

seven (adjective) *students* (noun)

the *student's* (adjective) *chair* (noun)

·*her* (adjective) *door* (noun)

Recognizing adjectives will help you recognize nouns—and vice-versa! Finally, you will want to recognize the adjectives' characteristics.

C. Characteristics:

1. Certain endings on adjectives enable us to make comparisons.

    Example 1:
    Andrea is a *pretty* girl.
    (We are talking about only one girl, so we use the plain form of the adjective, *pretty.*)

    Example 2:
    Betty, however, is *prettier* than Andrea.
    (Now we are talking about the comparison of two girls, so we use the comparative form, the *-er* form, *prettier.*)

    Example 3:
    But Priscilla is the *prettiest* of the three.
    (Since we are now comparing three, we must use the superlative form, the *-est* form, *prettiest.*)

We often misuse these three forms—usually substituting the *-est* form for the *-er* form. For instance, if you have only one brother and he is taller than you, then he is the *taller* of the two; you are the *shorter* (not *shortest*). If you have a sister two years younger than you and you have no other brothers or sisters, then you are the *older* child (not *oldest*) in your family. If, on the other hand, you have *two* siblings, both of whom are older than you, then you are the *youngest* of the three. To summarize:

one person	= pretty, short, old, young
one of *two* persons	= prettier, shorter, older, younger
one of *three* or more persons	= prettiest, shortest, oldest, youngest

The endings *-er* and *-est* will work for short adjectives, but if the adjective has three or more syllables, use another word instead of the ending:

pretty	prettier	prettiest
beautiful	more beautiful	most beautiful

Use *more* like *-er* and *most* like *-est*.

Of course, there are some words that have their own peculiar comparisons, but you are no doubt familiar with them. You would not say *good, gooder, goodest,* now, would you! So you recognize *good, better,* and *best* as the usual comparisons. But the point remains: comparisons are characteristic of adjectives.

2. Placement also helps to identify adjectives.

    a. Adjectives usually appear in front of the nouns they modify.

        Example:
        A *pretty* girl is like a melody.
        (*Pretty* describes *what kind* about the noun *girl*.)

    b. The adjective can appear after a linking verb. That adjective is called a predicate adjective.

        Example:
        She is *pretty*.
        (*Pretty* describes *what kind* about the noun *she* and comes after the linking verb *is*.)

PART IV: ADVERBS

A. **Definition:** An adverb modifies a verb, an adjective, or another adverb.

B. **Function:** An adverb will answer the following questions about verbs, adjectives, or other adverbs:

1. *Where?*

    Example 1:
    He walked *home*.
    (*Home* tells *where* about the verb *walked*.)

Example 2:
The lumberjack cut *down* the tree.
(*Down* tells *where* about the verb *cut.* That sentence could also read this way: The lumberjack cut the tree *down.* Adverbs are moveable!)

Hint:
Since adverbs are moveable, try that moving test when you do not know whether down *is an adverb or a preposition. Prepositions cannot be moved.*

> *Example 1:*
> The fireman ran *down* the hall.
> (Since we cannot say, "The fireman ran the hall down," we know that *down* is a preposition.)

> *Example 2:*
> The wrestler knocked *down* his opponent.
> (We can say, "The wrestler knocked his opponent down," so we know the moveable word is an adverb, not a preposition.)

2. *When?*

   Example 1:
   He walked to school *yesterday.*
   (*Yesterday* tells *when* about the verb *walked.*)

   Example 2:
   The bell rang *late.*
   (*Late* tells *when* about the the verb *rang.*)

3. *How?*

   Example 1:
   The aspen swayed *gently* in the wind.
   (*Gently* tells *how* about the verb *swayed.*)

   Example 2:
   The aspen swayed *very gently* in the wind.
   (*Very* tells *how* about the adverb *gently.*)

4. *To what extent?*

   Example 1:
   He tried *quite* hard to finish the job.
   (*Quite* tells *to what extent* about the adverb *hard. Hard* tells *how* about the verb *tried.*)

   Example 2:
   He was *absolutely* certain about the answer.
   (*Absolutely* tells *to what extent* about the predicate adjective *certain.*)

C. **Characteristics:** Adverbs have two characteristic endings that help identify them:

   1. Adverbs, like adjectives, can be compared using the endings -*er* and -*est* or the words *more* and *most.*

Example 1:
The men work *hard.*

Example 2:
The men worked *harder* today than they did yesterday.
(Comparison of how *hard* the men worked on *two* days requires the comparative, or *-er,* form.)

Example 3:
Of all the days in the week that they worked, the men worked *hardest* on Saturday.
(The comparison of how *hard* the men worked on *six* days requires the superlative *-est* form.)

Example 4:
The children behaved *properly.*

Example 5:
These children behaved *more properly* than those.
(Comparison of how *two* groups behaved requires the comparative, or *more,* form.)

Example 6:
Of the three groups of children, the neighbor's children behaved *most properly.*
(The comparison of how *three* groups behaved requires the superlative *most* form.)

Since both adjectives and adverbs have the characteristic of comparison, you will have to go back to consider *function* to distinguish between the two. Adjectives will make comparisons about *nouns.* Adverbs will make comparisons about *verbs, adjectives,* and other *adverbs.*

Consider, too, this additional characteristic ending of adverbs:

2.   Adverbs often end in *-ly.*

Example:
He worked rapid*ly,* ate hungri*ly,* and slept sound*ly.*

Warning:
Not all words that end in *-ly* are adverbs. Some are adjectives. Be sure to check function.

Example:
He was a *friendly* man who had a *burly* physique.
(*Friendly* tells what kind of *man* [noun], and *burly* tells what kind of *physique* [noun], so both are adjectives by *function.*)

PART V: PREPOSITIONS

A. **Definition:** A preposition shows the relationship of its object to another word in the sentence. (That definition probably does not help much, but don't give up yet!)

B. **Function:**   The preposition, with its object, functions as a single word.

Note:

To find the object of the preposition, ask *who?* or *what?* after the preposition.

> *Example 1:*
> The poodle frisked *through the room.*
> > *Ask:* through *what?*
> > *Answer:* through *the room*
>
> (*Room* is the object of the preposition *through.* The preposition and its object form the prepositional phrase *through the room. Through* shows the relationship between the noun *room* and the verb *frisked.*)

> *Example 2:*
> The terrier barked *at the frisky little poodle.*
> > *Ask:* at *who* or at *what?*
> > *Answer:* at *the poodle*
>
> (*Poodle* is the object of the preposition *at.* The prepositional phrase begins with the preposition and ends with its object: *at* (preposition) *the frisky little poodle* (object of the preposition). The phrase includes, therefore, any modifiers of the object. In the sentences above, *frisky* and *little* both modify *poodle* and so are part of the prepositional phrase.)

To summarize, then, the prepositional phrase functions as a single word. It functions in one of two ways:

1.   As an adjective

Example:
The girl *with red hair* is my friend.
(*With* shows the relationship of *hair* to *girl,* and *with red hair* tells *which* about the noun *girl.* The whole phrase *with red hair* functions as a single word, as an adjective modifying *girl.*)

2.   As an adverb

Example:
The girl who fell *into the bucket* of wet cement needs a hose.
(*Into* shows the relationship between *fell* and *bucket. Into the bucket* says *where* about *fell,* and the whole phrase functions as a single word, as an adverb modifying the verb *fell.* Incidentally, *of wet cement* functions as an adjective describing *what kind* about *bucket.*)

C. **Characteristics:**   The following characteristics indicate prepositions:

1.   A preposition will always be followed by an object, which must be a noun. (Remember, *all* objects are nouns.)

Since prepositions are rather peculiar words that we use frequently, you really need to be able to recognize them easily. Prepositional phrases cause all sorts of problems later if you fail to learn to recognize them. Since the definition does not really help to identify prepositions easily, think of this final characteristic, peculiar though it may be, as one that will help you find those prepositions easily:

2. A preposition is "any place a rat can run." (The preposition *of* is the only exception!)

Strange? Yes, but look at the following list of prepositions, written here with objects (forming prepositional phrases), to see how this strange idea works:

A rat can run *about* the room,
above the window,
or *across* your desk
any time *after* 8:00,
even *against* your wishes.
He can run *along* your foot,
among your books,
or *around* your shoulders
at an easy pace.
That same rat can run *before* your very eyes
or *behind* your back,
below the bookcase
or *beneath* the door.
He can run *beside* your notebook,
between your boots,
or *beyond* your reach
by the file cabinet.
This wily little rat can run *down* your arm
during third-period class
except on Saturdays and Sundays
for many hours
from now *until* 3:30!
He can also run *from* the exterminator
in a panic
into hiding
like a flash
of lightning.
He can run *off* the window ledge
on the east side *of* the room,
over the wall,
through the meadow and *to* the woods
toward Grandmother's house!
He can even run *under* her door,
and *up* the attic stairs
with great haste
without a sound.
He can run *as well as* walk
as far as Tennessee
in spite of his short legs
because of his great energy.

And so, you see, some prepositions are even made of more than one word; but the rat, ambitious little creature that he is, can still run!

REVIEW

You now have the basic information about the five parts of speech. Use the following sentences as a review to see if you understand this basic information. Determine the part of speech of the italicized word. Answers follow. When you have finished, check your answers; try to figure out *why* you went wrong—*if* you did.

Sentences

1. The football fans cheered the first *down*.

2. *Down* jackets keep the wearer quite warm in very cold weather.

3. Climbing carefully *down* the ladder, he felt more and more relief as he neared the bottom.

4. The champion wrestler will *down* his opponent easily.

5. That little imp knocked *down* my carefully stacked dominoes!

6. The manager is working *outside* his realm of authority.

7. As he stepped *outside,* the wind blasted him in the face.

8. To conserve energy, we planned to insulate all the *outside* walls.

9. Those two boys really *like* baseball!

10. The Wargels painted their house green; we plan to paint ours in a *like* manner.

11. At my suggestion of a date at the movies, her face lit up *like* a neon sign.

12. I watched as my colleague *neared* the podium.

13. The burglary occurred *near* the intersection of Third and Main Streets.

14. Time draws *near*!

15. Having been involved in a *near* accident, Joyce drives more carefully now.

16. The winter's supply of firewood is *nearly* gone.

17. The horse *nearing* the finish line is being ridden by the youngest jockey here.

18. History studies the *past*.

19. His *past* actions are a good indication of what to expect in the future.

20. Thank goodness, I *passed* the course!

21. Yesterday, my sister slept *past* noon.

22. The jogger runs *past* the post office every afternoon.

Solutions

1. *Noun.* The clues are the article *the* and the adjective *first. Down* functions as a direct object of the verb *cheered.*

2. *Adjective.* It describes *what kind of* about the noun *jacket.*

3. *Preposition.* A rat can run *down the ladder. Down* has a noun-object: *ladder.*

4. *Verb. Will* is a helping verb, so its presence indicates a verb phrase.

5. *Adverb.* It tells *where* about *knocked,* the verb. (If you were tempted to call this one a preposition, note that the sentence can be rearranged to read, "That little imp knocked my carefully stacked dominoes down." Because *down* can be moved about in the sentence, you can guess that it functions as an adverb.)

6. *Preposition.* A rat can run *outside his realm of authority*! *Realm* is a noun, the object of the preposition.

7. *Adverb.* It tells *where* about the verb *stepped.*

8. *Adjective.* It tells *which ones* about the noun *walls.*

9. *Verb.* You can change the time: Yesterday, those boys really *liked* baseball.

10. *Adjective. Like* tells *what kind of* about the noun *manner.*

11. *Preposition. Like* has a noun object: *sign.* The whole phrase tells *how* about *lit.*

12. *Verb.* You can change the time: Tomorrow my colleague *will near* the podium.

13. *Preposition.* A rat can run *near the intersection. Intersection,* a noun, is the object of the preposition *near.* As a phrase, *near the intersection* tells *where* about the verb *occurred.*

14. *Adverb. Near* tells *where* about *draws,* the verb.

15. *Adjective. Near* tells *what kind of* about the noun *accident.*

16. *Adverb.* The *-ly* ending is a clue. So is the fact that *nearly* tells *to what extent* about *is gone,* the verb.

17. *Adjective.* Bet you goofed on that one! Did you call it a verb? *Nearing* here tells *which* about *horse:* the one *nearing the finish line.*

18. *Noun. The* is the first clue that you have a noun. *Past* also functions as the object of the verb *studies.*

19. *Adjective. Past* tells *which ones* about *actions.*

20. *Verb.* The *-ed* ending is a clue, but you need to see if that word will, in fact, change time: Tomorrow, I *will pass* the course.

21. *Preposition.* Can't a rat run *past noon?*

22. *Preposition.* Rats can run *past the post office,* too!

Now try these nonsense sentences. By applying all the clues, you should be able to determine the part of speech of each of the words in these sentences! When you finish, check your answers with those below.

Sentences

1. The quargle fotterstadt with yankop in its zedtop doppled lommily down the prufhoth.

2. A rewant at the moldud prampted the wobats.

3. After gundernt, an uprezeted flingle was omkled into the vifertt.

4. A langly priffert under the croddertz humphered and wekkened ikingly until eddstodt.

5. During a dedderft in the bockfert, the okkendult's caedt is gunrothing.

Solutions

Sentence 1:

> *The—article,* determines that a noun follows
>
> *quargle—adjective,* modifies *fotterstadt*
>
> *fotterstadt—noun,* subject
>
> *with—preposition*
>
> *yankop—noun,* object of the preposition *with*
>
> *in—preposition*
>
> *its—adjective,* modifies *zedtop*
>
> *zedtop—noun,* object of the preposition *in*
>
> *doppled—verb*
>
> *lommily—adverb,* modifies the verb *doppled*
>
> *down—preposition*
>
> *the—article,* determines that a noun follows
>
> *prufhoth—noun,* object of the preposition *down*

Sentence 2:

> *A—article,* determines that a noun follows
>
> *rewant—noun,* subject
>
> *at—preposition*
>
> *the—article,* determines that a noun follows
>
> *moldud—noun,* object of preposition *at*
>
> *prampted—verb*

the—*article*, determines that a noun follows

wobats—*noun*, object of the verb *prampted*

Sentence 3:

After—*preposition*

gundernt—*noun*, object of the preposition *after*

an—*article*, determines that a noun follows

uprezeted—*adjective*, modifies *flingle*

flingle—*noun*, subject

was omkled—*verb*

into—*preposition*

the—*article*, determines that a noun follows

vifertt—*noun*, object of the preposition *into*

Sentence 4:

A—*article*, determines that a noun follows

langly—*adjective*, modifies *priffert*

priffert—*noun*, subject

under—*preposition*

the—*article*, determines that a noun follows

croddertz—*noun*, object of the preposition *under*

humphered—*verb*

and—*joining word*

wekkened—*verb*

ikingly—*adverb*, modifies verbs *humphered* and *wekkened*

until—*preposition*

eddstodt—*noun*, object of the preposition *until*

Sentence 5:

During—*preposition*

a—*article*, determines that a noun follows

dedderft—*noun*, object of the preposition *during*

in—*preposition*

the—*article*, determines that a noun follows

bockfert—*noun*, object of the preposition *in*

the—*article*, determines that a noun follows

okkendult's—*possessive noun;* functions as adjective; modifies *caedt*

caedt—noun, subject

*is gunrothing—*verb

If you made reasonable progress with these sentences, you are well on your way toward mastery. Keep in mind that Chapter 2, *Parts of the Sentence,* will help you sort out and understand some specifics that may at present be unclear.

2

PARTS OF THE SENTENCE

A SENTENCE - ATTACK PLAN

Because it is important later in being able to determine correct usage, you must be able to find the major parts of the sentence:

subject

verb

direct object

indirect object

predicate word

objective complement

There are eight steps to a sentence-attack plan that will help you recognize the principal parts of the sentence.

Step 1: Mark out all the prepositional phrases. Remember that the prepositional phrase is the preposition *plus* the noun that is its object *plus* any words in between. (The words in between are modifiers of the object.) In other words:

preposition
+
modifiers   } = prepositional phrase
+
noun [object]

Since prepositional phrases can function only as modifiers, they cannot function as any major part of the sentence. As a result, you will keep yourself out of trouble by eliminating them from the beginning.

Example:
A dish of grapes was sitting on the dining room table.
After the prepositional phrases are marked out: A dish . . . was sitting. . . .

Note:
By eliminating *of grapes,* the prepositional phrase, you will eliminate any confusion between the nouns later when you must select the subject of the sentence.

25

Step 2:   Find the word that changes *time*. That word will be the verb. (Be sure to find the whole verb phrase.) Remember that to make finding the verb easier, you can add the words *yesterday* or *tomorrow* in front of the sentence.

Example:
A dish of grapes was sitting on the dining-room table.
Step 1:   A dish . . . was sitting. . . .
Step 2:   A dish was sitting.
           Tomorrow, a dish *will be* sitting.
           (Helper verbs *will* and *be* are joined with the main verb, *sitting*.)
           Was sitting is the whole verb.

Step 3:   Determine whether the verb is an action verb or a linking verb. (You may need to review verb characteristics in Chapter 1, Part II, Section C.)

Example:
Some of the students in the hall are friends of mine.
Step 1:   Some . . . are friends. . . .
Step 2:   Some are friends.
           Yesterday, some *were* friends.
           Are is the verb.
Step 3:   *Are* is a linking verb. (It is one of the verbs *to be* that are always linking.)

Step 4:   Ask *who?* or *what?* in front of the verb to determine the subject.

Example:
Most of the people at the circus reacted with surprise at the clown's antics.
Step 1:   Most . . . reacted. . . .
Step 2:   Most *reacted*.
Step 3:   *Reacted* is an action verb.
Step 4:   *Who* or *what* reacted?
           Answer: *most*
           Most is the subject.

Two warnings are necessary as we talk about subjects:

Warning 1:
Sometimes the subject does not appear in front of the verb. Asking *who?* or *what?* in front of the verb will still determine the subject, but you may have to look *after* the verb in the sentence in order to find the answer.

Example:
Onto the field ran the coach and his team.
Step 1:   . . .ran the coach and his team.
Step 2:   Ran the coach and his team.
           Tomorrow *will run* the coach and his team.
           Ran is the verb.
Step 3:   *Ran* is an action verb.

Step 4: *Who* or *what* ran?
Answer: *coach and team.*
Coach and *team* are the subjects.

Warning 2:
The words *here* and *there* can never be subjects. (They tell *where* and usually function as adverbs.) In sentences that begin with *here* or *there,* you will have to look *after* the verb to find the subject.

Example:
There are two bowls of shelled pecans in the cabinet.
Step 1: There are two bowls. . . .
Step 2: There are two bowls.
Yesterday, there *were* two bowls.
Are is the verb.
Step 3: *Are* is a linking verb.
Step 4: *Who* or *what* are?
Answer: *bowls* (*Here* and *there* can never be subjects.)
Bowls is the subject.

Step 5: If you have a *linking* verb, skip to Step 8. If you have an *action* verb, ask *who?* or *what?* after the verb to find the direct object. (Remember, the direct object must be a noun.)

Example:
A few of the children brought their toys with them to the birthday party for my little brother.
Step 1: A few . . . brought their toys. . . .
Step 2: A few brought their toys.
Tomorrow, a few *will bring* their toys.
Brought is the verb.
Step 3: *Brought* is an action verb.
Step 4: *Who* or *what* brought?
Answer: *few* (subject)
Step 5: Since *brought* is an action verb, ask:
Few brought *who* or *what?*
Answer: *toys*
Toys is the direct object.

Two warnings follow:

Warning 1:
Not all action verbs will have a direct object. Consider, for example, the sentence in the example for Step 4: *Most of the people at the circus reacted with surprise at the clown's antics.* After all the prepositional phrases were crossed out, nothing was left except *most reacted. Most* is the subject, and *reacted* is the verb. Even though *reacted* is an action verb, there is nothing to answer the questions *who?* or *what?* for the direct object. Consider this additional example:

Example:
The dark, ominous clouds moved steadily toward us from the western horizon.
Step 1: The dark, ominous clouds moved steadily. . . .

Step 2:   The dark, ominous clouds moved steadily.
          Tomorrow, the dark, ominous clouds *will move* steadily.
          Moved is the verb.
Step 3:   *Moved* is an action verb.
Step 4:   *Who* or *what* moved?
          Answer: *clouds* (subject)
Step 5:   Since *moved* is an action verb, ask:
          Clouds moved *who* or *what*?
          Answer: none (*Steadily* tells *how*, not *who* or *what*.)
          There is no direct object.

Warning 2:
There can be no direct object after a linking verb.

Example:
The water seemed deep along the bank.
Step 1:   The water seemed deep. . . .
Step 2:   The water seemed deep.
          Tomorrow, the water *will seem* deep.
          Seemed is the verb.
Step 3:   *Seemed* is a linking verb.
Step 4:   *Who* or *what* seemed?
          Answer: *water* (subject)
Step 5:   You cannot complete this step because the verb is *linking*. Go to Step 8.

Note:
If you did ask the questions for the direct object (water seemed *who* or *what*?) you would get an answer: *deep*. But there are two problems here:

1.   You cannot have a direct object after a linking verb.

2.   *Deep* is not a noun. Direct objects must be nouns.

You can see, then, why Step 3 is so important. If you neglect to determine whether the verb is an action verb or a linking verb, you will probably get into trouble at Step 5.

Sometimes you will find a sentence that has words that seem to answer both *who*? and *what*? after the verb. Compare these two sentences:

Example 1:
John bought ice cream and cookies.
John bought *what*?
Answer: *ice cream and cookies*
(You have two direct objects joined with *and*.)

Example 2:
John bought Sue candy.
John bought *who* or *what*?
Answer: *Sue and candy*?
(It appears that *Sue* answers *who*?, and *candy* answers *what*? But did John buy Sue? Not quite! That leads us to Step 6.)

Step 6:   If you have a direct object, ask *to whom*? or *for whom*? to find the indirect object. You cannot have an indirect object if there is no direct object.

Example:
For Christmas, Barbara bought her family airline tickets to England.
Step 1: . . . Barbara bought her family airline tickets. . . .
Step 2: Barbara bought her family airline tickets.
Tomorrow, Barbara *will buy* her family airline tickets.
Bought is the verb.
Step 3: *Bought* is an action verb.
Step 4: *Who* or *what* bought?
Answer: *Barbara* (subject)
Step 5: Barbara bought *who* or *what*?
Answer: *tickets* (direct object)
Step 6: Since we have a direct object, ask:
Barbara bought tickets *to whom* or *for whom*?
Answer: *family*
Family is the indirect object.

Note:
In Step 5 you could have had two answers:
—Barbara bought *who?*
Answer: *family* (Of course, that does not really make sense. Barbara did not buy her family!)
—Barbara bought *what?*
Answer: *tickets*
Even though *family* was not a sensible answer for Step 5, if you were not thinking carefully, you could have stumbled at that point. So consider these three warnings:

Warning 1:
If there appear to be two words, one of which answers *who?* and another of which answers *what?*, the first one (which answers *who?*) is the indirect object, and the second one (which answers *what?*) is the direct object.

> *Example:*
> Laura taught her classmates a new dance step.
> Step 5: Laura taught *who* or *what*?
> Answer: *step* (direct object)
> Step 6: Laura taught step *to whom* or *for whom*?
> Answer: *classmates* (indirect object)
> *Classmates* answers *who?* and *step* answers *what?*, so the answer to *who?* is the indirect object and the answer to *what?* is the direct object.

Warning 2:
The indirect object will always appear in the sentence between the verb and the direct object. It cannot appear after the direct object. If the sentence pattern is

noun/verb/noun/noun

then the pattern may be

subject/verb/indirect object/direct object

(See Step 7 for a possible alternative pattern.)

Warning 3:
If the word *to* or *for* actually appears in front of the word you think is the indirect object, you have a prepositional phrase, not an indirect object. And you should have crossed out all prepositional phrases in Step 1!

Example:
Madelyn bought tickets for us for Saturday's concert.
Step 5:   Madelyn bought *who* or *what?*
          Answer: *tickets* (direct object)
Step 6:   Madelyn bought tickets *to whom* or *for whom?*
          Answer: none
The *for* in front of *us* makes *for us* a prepositional phrase. You can see once again the importance of Step 1. Be sure to eliminate all prepositional phrases!

Step 7:   If you have a direct object and you also have a word that renames or describes the direct object, you have an objective complement instead of an indirect object. The objective complement may be either a noun or an adjective. Although we do not use this sentence structure often, we need to recognize its existence.

Example 1:
The class elected Terry president.
Step 5:   Class elected *who* or *what?*
          Answer: *Terry* (direct object)
Step 7:   What word renames or describes *Terry?*
          Answer: *president*
          President is an objective complement.
          The noun *president* functions to rename the direct object *Terry.*

Note:
Since *Terry* and *president* both answer the questions for the direct object, simply choose the first one for the direct object and the second one for the objective complement. The sentence pattern here is the same as for the indirect object:

noun/verb/noun/noun

But now the pattern is

subject/verb/direct object/objective complement

Example 2:
He called me silly.
Step 5:   He called *who* or *what?*
          Answer: *me* (direct object)
Step 7:   What word renames or describes *me?*
          Answer: *silly*
          Silly is an objective complement.
          The adjective *silly* functions to describe the direct object *me.*

Example 3:
The coach thought the play a brilliant maneuver.
Step 5:   Coach thought *who* or *what?*
          Answer: *play*

Step 7:   What word renames or describes *play*?
          Answer: *maneuver* (objective complement)

Step 8:   If you have a linking verb, the word that answers *who?* or *what?* after
          the verb is the predicate word. The predicate word may be a noun or an
          adjective.

          Note:
          You are asking the same questions that you did in Step 5, but now you
          are asking them after a *linking* verb, not an action verb.

          Example 1:
          The chocolate cake on the right end of the table is especially well
          decorated.
          Step 1:   The chocolate cake . . . is especially well decorated.
          Step 2:   The chocolate cake is especially well decorated.
                    Yesterday, the chocolate cake *was* especially well decorated.
                    Is is the verb.
          Step 3:   *Is* is a linking verb.
          Step 4:   *Who* or *what is?*
                    Answer: *cake* (subject)
          Step 5:   If you have a linking verb, skip to Step 8.
          Step 8:   Cake is *who* or *what?*
                    Answer: *decorated*
                    Decorated is the predicate word. It is a predicate adjective.

          Example 2:
          The red-haired boy in the third seat probably will be valedictorian of his
          class.
          Step 1:   The red-haired boy . . . probably will be valedictorian. . . .
          Step 2.   The red-haired boy probably will be valedictorian.
                    Yesterday, the red-haired boy probably *would have been*
                    valedictorian.
                    Will be is the verb.
          Step 3:   *Will be* is a linking verb.
          Step 4:   *Who* or *what* will be?
                    Answer: *boy* (subject)
          Step 5:   If you have a linking verb, skip to Step 8.
          Step 8:   Boy will be *who* or *what?*
                    Answer: *valedictorian*
                    Valedictorian is the predicate word. It is a predicate noun.

Compound Parts

   Now that you have considered the eight steps of the sentence-attack plan,
you need to deal with one more concept that can apply to all eight steps:

          Any part of the sentence can be compound. The compound parts may
          be joined by the words *and, but, or,* or *nor.*

The following examples illustrate:

Step 1: Compound object of the preposition

Example:
The sunbeams reflected through the *goblets and vases* in the jewelry store's *windows and showcases.*

Step 2: Compound verb

Example:
Shop owners *advertise* their products *and solicit* our business.

Step 3: Compound verb, one of which is an action verb and the other of which is a linking verb

Example:
The track team *represented* young people from many backgrounds *and was* a melting-pot for their differences.
(*Represented* is an action verb and *was* is a linking verb.)

Step 4: Compound subject

Example:
Most of her friends *and* a few *acquaintances* showed up for the open-house in her honor.

Step 5: Compound direct object

Example:
The chemist was awarded a bronze *plaque and* a $1000 cash *prize* for his work in cancer research.

Step 6: Compound indirect object

Example:
The guide offered *Dan or me* a free two-day fishing trip.

Step 7: Compound objective complement

Example:
In desperation, the mayor assigned Mr. McGilles chief *arbitrator and* mayoral *representative* in the labor dispute.

Step 8: Compound predicate-adjective

Example:
That cold lemonade tasted *sweet but refreshing.*

Sometimes a sentence can have several compound parts:

Example:
The grounds keeper and his assistants built the young boys and girls a long-needed bicycle path and foot trail, and, as a result, are both excited and gratified by the children's positive reaction and steady use of the new facilities.

Step 1: compound object of preposition:
reactions and *use* (also *facilities*)

Step 2:   compound verb:
          built and *are*

Step 3:   compound verb, one action and the other linking:
          built (action) and *are* (linking)

Step 4:   compound subject:
          keeper and *assistants*

Step 5:   compound direct object:
          path and *trail*

Step 6:   compound indirect object:
          boys and *girls*

Step 8:   compound predicate adjectives:
          excited and *gratified*

Summary of the Sentence-Attack Plan

Step 1:   Mark out the prepositional phrase.

Step 2:   Find the verb, the word that changes time.

Step 3:   Determine whether the verb is an action verb or a linking verb.

Step 4:   Ask *who?* or *what?* in front of the verb to determine the subject. (*Who* or *what* [verb]?)

Step 5:   If you have a linking verb, skip to Step 8. If you have an action verb, ask *who?* or *what?* after the verb to find the direct object. ([Subject] [verb] *who* or *what?*)

Step 6:   If you have a direct object, ask *to whom?* or *for whom?* after the direct object to find the indirect object.

Step 7:   Any word that renames or describes the direct object is the objective complement.

Step 8:   If you have a linking verb, ask *who?* or *what?* after the verb to find the predicate word.

REVIEW

For review, consider the following questions about the general ideas in the sentence-attack plan. Check your answers with those at the end of these questions. No cheating, now!

Questions

1. Can you have a compound subject?
2. Can you have a direct object after a linking verb?
3. Must you have an indirect object after a direct object?
4. Do action verbs take predicate words?
5. Will most linking verbs have predicate words?
6. Will all action verbs have direct objects?
7. Can you have an indirect object without a direct object?
8. Can a sentence have both a predicate word and a direct object?
9. Can the verb be more than one word?
10. Can there be more than one verb in a sentence?
11. Can there be both a linking verb and an action verb in the same sentence?
12. Can direct objects appear after action verbs?
13. Can there be two direct objects in a sentence?
14. Can a sentence have both a direct object and an objective complement?
15. Can a sentence have both a direct object and an indirect object?
16. Must a sentence have a subject?
17. Will the subject appear in front of the verb?
18. Will all sentences have a verb?
19. Will all sentences have either a direct object or a predicate word?
20. Are all subjects, direct objects, indirect objects, predicate words, and objective complements nouns?

Answers

1. *Yes. Example:* My *sister* and *Georgette* are going shopping.
2. *No.* Direct objects must follow action verbs.
3. *No.* A direct object may exist without an indirect object.
4. *No.* Predicate words follow linking verbs.

34

5. *Yes.* Most linking verbs will have a predicate word, but sometimes that predicate word is implied. *Example:* Is Sue your sister? Yes, she is. (*My sister* are the implied predicate words.)

6. *No. Example:* Joanne jogs after school every day. Joanne jogs *who* or *what?* Answer: none.

7. *No.* There must be a direct object before there can be an indirect object.

8. *Yes,* but only if there are *both* an action verb and a linking verb.

9. *Yes.* The verb often has helpers.

10. *Yes. Example:* Barbara *bought* and *delivered* the flowers herself.

11. *Yes. Example:* The young athlete *ran* seven miles and *was* exhausted.

12. *Yes.* Not every action verb, however, must have a direct object.

13. *Yes. Example:* Our members read both newspaper *reports* and magazine *articles* about the dispute.

14. *Yes.* The objective complement renames or describes the direct object, so there must be a direct object before there can be an objective complement.

15. *Yes.* A sentence must have a direct object before it can have an indirect object, but the direct object may exist without an indirect object.

16. *Yes,* of course!

17. *Not always.* Remember that *here* and *there,* for instance, cannot be subjects; the subject will have to come after the verb in that case. There are other situations, too, of course, in which the subject comes later.

18. *Yes!*

19. *No.* Since an action verb may exist without a direct object and since, in some cases, linking verbs have only implied predicate words, a sentence may exist—and often does, in fact—with only a subject and a verb.

20. *No.* Predicate words and objective complements may be nouns or adjectives.

Now that you have reviewed the sentence-attack plan, try applying the eight steps to the following sentences. You will need to apply, also, the information you learned in Chapter 1. Label the following items in these sentences:

subject

verb

direct object, if any

indirect object, if any

objective complement, if any

predicate word, if any

When you finish, check your answers on the following pages.

Sentences

1. The professor, with some help from his niece, found his car keys behind the cushion.

2. A couple of my friends seemed especially pleased with their respective successes at the track meet.

3. One of the cheerleaders fell during the half-time show and twisted his left ankle.

4. The mayor sent the City Council her ideas for improving city traffic flow.

5. We bought three back issues of *National Geographic* for your use.

6. Do you really understand these solutions to the problem?

7. The essay-contest winners were a boy in my class and a girl in the twelfth grade.

8. Funds from the state government made local road improvements possible.

9. With his courage, he will win a medal for bravery.

10. Most young speakers appear nervous but usually steel themselves with determination.

11. The basketball referee called the player's action a personal foul.

12. Some of these civic-minded people have been buying their out-of-town friends souvenirs from our city.

Solutions

Sentence 1:   The professor, with some help from his niece, found his car keys behind the cushion.

Step 1:   The professor . . . found his car keys . . . .

Step 2:   The professor found his car keys.
Tomorrow, the professor *will find* his car keys.
Found is the verb.

Step 3:   *Found* is an action verb.

Step 4:   *Who* or *what* found?
Answer: *professor* (subject)

Step 5:   Professor found *who* or *what?*
Answer: *keys* (direct object)

Step 6:   Professor found keys *to whom* or *for whom?*
Answer: none

Sentence 2:   A couple of my friends seemed especially pleased with their respective successes at the track meet.

Step 1:   A couple . . . seemed especially pleased. . . .

Step 2:   A couple seemed especially pleased.
Tomorrow, a couple *will seem* especially pleased.
Seemed is the verb.

Step 3:   *Seemed* is a linking verb.

Step 4:   *Who* or *what* seemed?
Answer: *couple* (subject)

Step 5:   If you have a linking verb, skip to Step 8.

Step 8:   Couple seemed *who* or *what?*
Answer: *pleased* (predicate word)

Sentence 3:   One of the cheerleaders fell during the half-time show and twisted his left ankle.

Step 1:   One . . . fell . . . and twisted his left ankle.

Step 2:   One fell and twisted his left ankle.
Tomorrow, one *will fall* and *twist* his left ankle.
Fell and *twisted* are the verbs.

Step 3:   *Fell* and *twisted* are both action verbs.

Step 4:   *Who* or *what* fell and twisted?
Answer: *one* (subject)

Step 5:   One fell *who* or *what?*
Answer: none
One twisted *who* or *what?*
Answer: *ankle* (direct object)

Step 6:   One twisted ankle *to whom* or *for whom?*
Answer: none

Sentence 4:   The mayor sent the City Council her ideas for improving city traffic flow.

Step 1:   The mayor sent the City Council her ideas. . . .

Step 2:   The mayor sent the City Council her ideas.
Tomorrow, the mayor *will send* the City Council her ideas.
Sent is the verb.

Step 3:   *Sent* is an action verb.

Step 4:   *Who* or *what* sent?
Answer: *mayor* (subject)

Step 5:   Mayor presented *who* or *what?*
Answer: *ideas* (direct object)

Step 6:   Mayor presented ideas *to whom* or *for whom?*
Answer: *City Council* (indirect object)

Sentence 5:   We bought three back issues of *National Geographic* for your use.

Step 1:   We bought three back issues. . . .

Step 2:   We bought three back issues.
Tomorrow, we *will buy* three back issues.
Bought is the verb.

Step 3:   *Bought* is an action verb.

Step 4: *Who* or *what* bought?
Answer: *we* (subject)

Step 5: We bought *who* or *what?*
Answer: *issues* (direct object)

Step 6: We bought issues *to whom* or *for whom?*
Answer: none (Remember, *for your use* is a prepositional phrase.)

Sentence 6: Do you really understand these solutions to the problem?

Step 1: Do you really understand these solutions. . . .

Step 2: Do you really understand these solutions?
Yesterday, *did* you really *understand* these solutions?
Do understand is the verb.
(Did you remember that *do* is usually a helping verb?)

Step 3: *Do understand* is an action verb.

Step 4: *Who* or *what* do understand?
Answer: *you* (subject)

Step 5: You do understand *who* or *what?*
Answer: *solutions* (direct object)

Step 6: You do understand solutions *to whom* or *for whom?*
Answer: none
(You didn't answer with *problems,* did you? Remember, you crossed that out in the prepositional phrase in Step 1.)

Sentence 7: The essay-contest winners were a boy in my class and a girl in the twelfth grade.

Step 1: The essay-contest winners were a boy . . . and a girl. . . .

Step 2: The essay-contest winners were a boy and a girl.
Tomorrow, the essay-contest winners *will be* a boy and a girl.
Were is the verb.

Step 3: *Were* is a linking verb.

Step 4: *Who* or *what* were?
Answer: *winners* (subject)

Step 5: If you have a linking verb, skip to Step 8.

Step 8: Winners were *who* or *what?*
Answer: *boy and girl* (compound predicate words)

Sentence 8: Funds from the state government made local road improvements possible.

Step 1: Funds . . . made local road improvements possible.

Step 2: Funds made local road improvements possible.
Tomorrow, funds *will make* local road improvements possible.
Made is the verb.

Step 3: *Made* is an action verb.

Step 4: *Who* or *what* made?
Answer: *funds* (subject)

Step 5: Funds made *who* or *what?*
Answer: *improvements* (direct object)

Step 6: Funds made improvements *to whom* or *for whom?*
Answer: none

Step 7: What word renames or describes the direct object?
Answer: *possible* (objective complement)

Sentence 9: With his courage, he will win a medal for bravery.

Step 1: . . . he will win a medal. . . .

Step 2: He will win a medal.
Yesterday, he *won* a medal.
Will win is the verb.

Step 3: *Will win* is an action verb.

Step 4: *Who* or *what* will win?
Answer: *he* (subject)

Step 5: He will win *who* or *what?*
Answer: *medal* (direct object)

Step 6: He will win medal *to whom* or *for whom?*
Answer: none

Sentence 10: Most young speakers appear nervous but usually steel themselves with determination.

Step 1: Most young speakers appear nervous but usually steel themselves. . . .

Step 2: Most young speakers appear nervous but usually steel themselves.
Tomorrow, most young speakers *will appear* nervous but usually *will steel* themselves.
Appear and *steel* are the verbs.

Step 3: *Appear* is a linking verb. (Substitute *are* to test the verb).
Steel is an action verb.

Step 4: *Who* or *what* appear?
Answer: *speakers* (subject)
Who or *what* steel?
Answer: *speakers* (subject)

Step 5: (Here is the tricky part. You have *both* an action verb and a linking verb. So you will need to do Step 5 with the verb *steel* and skip to Step 8 with the verb *appear.*)
Speakers steel *who* or *what?*
Answer: *themselves* (direct object)

Step 6: Speakers steel themselves *to whom* or *for whom?*
Answer: none

Step 8: Speakers appear *who* or *what?*
Answer: *nervous* (predicate word)

Sentence 11: The basketball referee called the player's action a personal foul.

Step 1: The basketball referee called the player's action a personal foul. (no prepositional phrases)

Step 2: The basketball referee called the player's action a personal foul.
Tomorrow, the basketball referee *will call* the player's action a personal foul.
Called is the verb.

Step 3: *Called* is an action verb.

Step 4: *Who* or *what* called?
Answer: *referee* (subject)

Step 5: Referee called *who* or *what?*
Answer: *action* (direct object)
(Since there appear to be two answers to the question, we know that we need to go on to Step 7.)

Step 7: What word renames or describes the direct object?
Answer: *foul* (objective complement)

Sentence 12: Some of these civic-minded people have been buying their out-of-town friends souvenirs from our city.

Step 1: Some . . . have been buying their out-of-town friends souvenirs. . . .

Step 2: Some have been buying their out-of-town friends souvenirs.
Yesterday, some *had been buying* their out-of-town friends souvenirs.
Have been buying is the verb.

Step 3: *Have been buying* is an action verb.

Step 4: *Who* or *what* have been buying?
Answer: *some* (subject)

Step 5: Some have been buying *who* or *what?*
Answer: *souvenirs* (direct object)
(Remember, they did not buy their friends!)

Step 6: Some have been buying souvenirs *to whom* or *for whom?*
Answer: *friends* (indirect object)

II

USAGE

3

AGREEMENT OF SUBJECT AND VERB

Now that you have grasped the basics of general "grammar," we are ready to talk about the real problems with writing and speaking: usage.

Agreement of subject and verb is, for the most part, a natural speech-pattern. Most of us grew up learning to say "The boy walks" and "The boys walk." We would never say "The boy walk" or "They walks." Sometimes, however, problem situations occur in which our "natural" patterns defeat us. These situations are what we need to talk about in this chapter.

BASIC PREMISES

Let us start with three basic premises:

1. Subjects can be singular or plural.

    Examples:
    The *apple* (singular) is rotten.
    The *apples* (plural) are rotten.

2. Verbs can be singular or plural.

    Examples:
    The child *talks* (singular) constantly.
    The children *talk* (plural) constantly.

    Note:
    Subjects add *-s* to form the *plural,* and verbs add *-s* to form the *singular.*
    Apple is singular. *Talks* is singular. *Apples* is plural. *Talk* is plural.

3. Subjects must agree in number with their verbs. Singular subjects must have singular verbs. Plural subjects must have plural verbs.

    Examples:
    He (singular subject) *walks* (singular verb).
    They (plural subject) *walk* (plural verb).

With these basic premises in mind, let us now consider the problems that occur in subject-verb agreement:

PROBLEMS

Problem 1: A problem occurs when the writer is confused about choosing the subject. Since the verb must agree with its subject, not recognizing the subject will result in a glaring error! (A review of Chapter 2 may help here.) Three specific situations seem to cause the greatest problems:

Situation A: Sometimes the writer has difficulty locating the subject when words come between the subject and its verb. These words may be prepositional phrases, verbal phrases, or clauses. Such words cause a problem because the writer's "natural" patterns make him want the verb to agree with the nearest noun—which may not be the subject.

Example 1:
The box of apples is beginning to rot.
(*Is beginning* must agree with its subject *box,* not with *apples* in the prepositional phrase.)

Example 2:
The cars, washed and shined with care, sit ready for the parade.
(*Sit* must agree with its subject *cars.* The verbal phrase *washed and shined with care* cannot alter the subject-verb agreement.)

Example 3:
Those motorcycles that roar up and down the street cause disturbance for the hospital.
(*Cause* must agree with its subject *motorcycles.* The clause *that roar up and down the street* cannot alter the subject-verb agreement.)

Warning:
Some prepositional phrases logically make a subject appear to be plural:

with	as well as
along with	in addition to
together with	

But prepositional phrases *cannot* alter the noun-subject.

Example 1:
The doctor, together with his two assistants, is working desperately.
(*Is working* must agree with its subject *doctor.* The prepositional phrase *together with his two assistants* cannot alter the subject-verb agreement, even though logic wants you to call that verb plural.)

Example 2:
My neighbor, along with her two German shepherds, walks across the pasture daily to visit.
(*Walks* must agree with its subject *neighbor.* Do not let the prepositional phrase *along with her two German shepherds* interfere.)

Example 3:
The television set, in addition to the hot water heater and the furnace, was damaged by the lightning.
(Was agrees with the subject *set.* Ignore those prepositional phrases!)

Situation B: Sometimes the writer may have difficulty locating the subject when the subject comes after the verb. If, for instance, the sentence begins with *here* or *there,* the subject comes *after* the verb.

Example 1:
There are three seats empty.
(Seats *are.*)

Example 2:
Here is the letter I was looking for.
(Letter *is.*)

Other sentences may also have the subject appearing after the verb:

Example 1:
Into the office charge the supervisor and her assistant.
(Supervisor and assistant *charge.*)

Example 2:
Where are the old newspapers?
(Newspapers *are.*)

Example 3:
Who are the girl in the ski outfit and the girl in the tennis dress?
(Girl and girl *are.*)

Situation C: Sometimes the writer is confused by the choice of subject if the subject is singular and the predicate word is plural—or vice-versa. He may think the verb *sounds* wrong; but the verb must agree with its subject, not its predicate word.

Example 1:
Physical conditioning and mental attitude are the winning combination.
(Conditioning and attitude *are.*)

Example 2:
The winning combination is physical conditioning and mental attitude.
(Combination *is.*)

Problem 2: A problem occurs when indefinite pronouns appear. There are three groups of indefinite pronouns:

Group A: Indefinite pronouns that are always singular:

someone	*anyone*	*everyone*
somebody	*anybody*	*everybody*
each	*one*	*either*
nobody	*no one*	*neither*

The easiest way to remember these singular words is to think *single one* or *one* with each:

> *some* [single] *one*
>
> *some* [single] *body*
>
> *every* [single] *one*
>
> *each* [single one]
>
> *neither* [one]

Example 1:
Everyone in the classrooms is too warm to study effectively.
(Think, "every [single] one *is*.")

Example 2:
Neither of the mechanics wants to work on Sunday.
(Think, "neither [one] *wants*.")

Example 3:
Everybody seated in the last two rows resents being asked to move forward.
(Think, "every [single] body *resents*.")

Example 4:
Each of my friends calls me once a week.
(Think, "each [one] *calls*.")

Group B: Indefinite pronouns that are always plural:

> *several*
>
> *few*
>
> *both*
>
> *many*

These words are especially easy to remember since they all *mean* "more than one."

Example 1:
Both of the books require careful reading.
(Both *require*.)

Example 2:
Several of the fielders regularly run four or five miles a day.
(Several *run*.)

Group C: Indefinite pronouns that can be singular or plural:

> *some*   *all*
>
> *any*   *most*
>
> *none*

To determine whether these words are singular or plural, look at the prepositional phrase that follows.

Example 1:
Some of the sugar is on the floor.

(Since *some* can be singular or plural, look at *sugar* to decide: *sugar is.*)

Example 2:
Some of the apples are in the sink.
(Since *some* can be singular or plural, look at *apples* to decide: *apples are.*)

Problem 3: A problem occurs when there are compound subjects. Three kinds of compound situations occur:

Situation A: Two subjects joined by *and* will always take a plural verb:

1 and 1   = 2
doctor and nurse   *work*
1 and 2   = 3
doctor and nurses   *work*
2 and 1   = 3
doctors and nurse   *work*

Note:
Some peculiar combinations occur that are logically singular. For these, use the singular verb.

Example 1:
Peaches and cream is my favorite desert.

Example 2:
My sister and best friend is Mary Ann.

Situation B: Two singular subjects joined by *or* or *nor* will take a singular verb:

1 or 1   = 1
doctor or nurse   *works*
1 nor 1   = 0
doctor nor nurse   *works*

Situation C: A singular subject and a plural subject joined by *or* or *nor* will take a singular or plural verb, depending on which subject is nearer the verb:

1   or 2   = 2
doctor   or *nurses work*
2   or 1   = 1
doctors or *nurse works*
1   nor 2   = 2
doctor   nor *nurses work*
2   nor 1   = 1
doctors nor *nurse works*

Consider the following examples for all three compound-subject situations:

Example 1:
Neither Ellen *nor* her *cousins are* planning a vacation.
(1 nor 2 = 2)

Example 2:
Neither her cousins *nor Ellen is* planning a vacation.
(2 nor 1 = 1)

Example 3:
Both her cousins *and* Ellen *are* planning a vacation.
(2 and 1 = 3)

Example 4:
Ellen *or* her *cousin is* planning a vacation.
(1 or 1 = 1)

Problem 4: A problem occurs when the subject is a collective noun that can be singular or plural. Collective nouns are nouns that represent a group: *team, jury, cast, class, crew, audience.*

Situation A: Collective nouns are *singular* when the group works together as a unit.

Example 1:
The *team runs* enthusiastically onto the floor.
(The team works together as a unit.)

Example 2:
The *jury has reached* its verdict.
(The jury functions as a unit in reaching a verdict.)

Situation B: Collective nouns are *plural* when the members of the group are acting individually.

Example 1:
The *team are putting* on their uniforms.
(Each team member acts individually to put on his own uniform. If we said, "The team *is* putting on its uniform, we would have the entire team in one uniform! How unhandy!)

Example 2:
The *jury have argued* for three hours.
(Each individual jury member is presenting his point of view.)

Hint:
Often the meaning of the sentence will tell you whether the collective noun is singular or plural, but sometimes additional hints appear—like plural pronouns.

Example 1:
The jury reaches *its* decision after much deliberation.
(The singular *its* gave a hint that *jury* is singular.)

Example 2:
The crew take *their places* five minutes before curtain time.
(The plural *their* and *places* give a hint that *crew* is plural. Of course, the entire crew could not be in one spot anyway!)

Problem 5: A problem occurs when words look plural but are not. Three such situations occur.

Situation A: Some words end in -s but represent a single thing: *news, measles, mumps.* These words need singular verbs.

Example 1:
The six o'clock *news is* about to begin.

Example 2:
Measles sometimes *has* rather serious side effects.

Warning:
Some words end in -s and *seem* to represent a single thing, but there are two *parts* to that single thing. Then the verb is plural. Consider words like *pants, scissors, trousers, shears,* and *pliers.*

Example 1:
The *scissors are* on the desk.

Example 2:
Here *are* the *pliers.*

Situation B: Words that end in -ics are usually singular: *politics, mathematics, civics, ethics, economics, athletics.* These words are *singular* when they refer to a study, science, or practice.

Example 1:
Politics is an interesting avocation.

Example 2:
Mathematics is his favorite subject.

Example 3:
Economics is a course required for high-school graduation.

Warning:
These words are *plural* when they have modifiers in front of them.

Example 1:
His politics are somewhat divided.
(The singular modifier *his* makes *politics* plural.)

Example 2:
The *mathematics* of the tax return *are* flawless.
(*The* makes *mathematics* plural.)

Example 3:
The *school's athletics are* all for both males and females.
(The modifiers *the school's* make *athletics* plural.)

Situation C: Some words that have become part of our language retain their original foreign plural forms:

Singular	Plural
datum	data
alumnus	alumni
memorandum	memoranda

Because we usually see these words in the plural form, we sometimes forget the singular form and thereby use the wrong verb-form. Consider these examples:

Example 1:
The *data were collected* by a licensed agency.

Example 2:
The *memoranda are* easily *read and understood.*

Situation D: Titles that are plural still represent a single thing, so the title needs a singular verb.

Example 1:
Great Expectations presents universal themes for all of us to consider.

Example 2:
A Man for All Seasons is playing at our local theater.

Situation E: Some nouns in the plural form represent an amount, a fraction, or an element of time. Those nouns are considered *singular.*

Hint:
Try substituting the words that amount *for the phrase. If the substitution works, the phrase is singular. If you need to substitute with* that number, *for countable items, then the phrase is plural.*

Example 1:
Sixty minutes is too much time to spend eating.
(*That amount* of time is too much time to spend eating.)

Compare: *Sixty minutes seem* to be passing rapidly on the timer's clock! (*That number* of minutes—countable—is passing.)

Example 2:
Five dollars is what that hamburger costs.
(*That amount* is what that hamburger costs.)

Compare: *Five one-dollar bills are* all he had with him. (*That number* of bills—countable—is what he had.)

Example 3:
Three-fourths of the pie is gone.
(*That amount* of the pie is gone.)

Compare: *Three-fourths of the cars are* gone from the parking lot. (*That number* is gone. Cars are countable.)

Example 4:
Sixty pounds is an excessive weight to mail.
(*That amount* is an excessive weight.)

Compare: *Sixty pounds of cornmeal were sold* to sixty customers yesterday. (*That number* of pounds were sold.)

If you can master these five problems, chances are you will have little or no difficulty in using the correct verb form to agree with the subject.

REVIEW

Try the following sentences to test yourself for understanding of all ten rules. Check your answers with those that follow. Problem and situation references are given so that you can review anything you may not yet have mastered.

Sentences

1. An Indian headdress and two beaded moccasins (was/were) in the museum window.

2. The boss's memoranda (is/are) filed away safely.

3. The neighbor, along with three of his friends, (is/are) going to Canada for a fishing trip.

4. Few of the trees (lose/loses) their leaves in spring.

5. *Three Faces of Eve* (is/are) a study in psychology.

6. Someone in one of these neighborhoods (is/are) on the mayor's investigative committee.

7. His ethics (requires/require) scrutiny.

8. All his friends (wishes/wish) him well and hope that all happiness (is/are) his.

9. None of the sunshine (seeps/seep) into the inner part of the house.

10. Everybody (knows/know) his part!

11. We thought five dollars (was/were) a fair donation.

12. Neither of the young men (was/were) recognized for outstanding contributions.

13. Neither the managers nor the supervisor (understands/understand) the complexity of the situation.

14. The crew (was/were) working at their respective jobs.

15. The bowl of bananas (is/are) tempting.

16. Everyone in the room (sees/see) opportunity knocking.

17. The baby and his mother (is/are), according to all reports, doing well.

18. Any of the nails that you don't use (is/are) returnable.

19. Although it is usually thought of as a childhood disease, measles (is/are) even more serious as an adult disease.

20. Mathematics (is/are) his favorite subject.

21. I hope somebody (sings/sing) the national anthem.

22. His hobby (is/are) butterflies.

23. Neither the carpenter nor the cabinet maker (was/were) willing to build the fancy shelves.

51

24. Both (is/are) excellent lecturers.

25. The city's economics (is/are) unsettled.

26. The financial advisor, in addition to the City Council members, (plans/plan) to complete additional reports for the year's end.

27. Their team usually (has/have) a successful season.

28. Miss Altheide or her two nieces (plans/plan) to attend the card party.

29. Some students (is/are) hoping that some achievement (is/are) forthcoming.

30. His tractor, as well as the plows, discs, and drills, (needs/need) regular maintenance.

31. Oil lamps (is/are) a good source of light.

32. Either crickets or minnows (makes/make) good fishing bait.

33. Three-fourths of his chickens (is/are) good layers.

34. Onto the rodeo grounds (charges/charge) a wild bull.

35. Politics (enters/enter) nearly everyone's life.

36. Seven one-dollar bills (brings/bring) him luck, he thinks.

37. Two cats and a dog (sleeps/sleep) together at my house.

38. That tree, which has heart-shaped leaves, (is/are) especially ornamental.

39. *Sixty Minutes* usually (airs/air) on Sunday evening.

40. Neither the roll-top desk nor the two electric typewriters (belongs/belong) to him.

41. As soon as the data (is/are) collected, the administration can give the results.

42. Athletics (is/are) a major part of her life.

43. The cast (performs/perform) admirably.

44. Either the scrubber or the precipitator (is/are) not functioning properly at the power-generating plant.

45. There (is/are) three people waiting to talk with the Congressman.

Solutions

1. headdress and moccasins *were* (Problem 3, Situation A)

2. memoranda *are* (Problem 5, Situation C)

3. neighbor *is* (Problem 1, Situation A)

4. few *lose* (Problem 2, Group B)

5. *Three Faces of Eve is* (Problem 5, Situation D)

6. someone *is* (Problem 2, Group A)

7. ethics *require* (Problem 5, Situation B)

8. all (friends) *wish and hope* (Problem 2, Group C)
   all (happiness) *is* (Problem 2, Group C)

9. none (sunshine) *seeps* (Problem 2, Group C)

10. everybody *knows* (Problem 2, Group A)

11. five dollars (that amount) *was* (Problem 5, Situation E)

12. neither *was* (Problem 2, Group A)

13. neither managers nor supervisor *understands* (Problem 3, Situation C)

14. crew *were* at *their* jobs (Problem 4, Situation B)

15. bowl *is* (Problem 1, Situation A)

16. everyone *sees* (Problem 2, Group A)

17. baby and mother *are* (Problem 3, Situation A)

18. any (nails) *are* (Problem 2, Group C)

19. measles *is* (Problem 5, Situation A)

20. mathematics *is* (Problem 5, Situation B)

21. somebody *sings* (Problem 2, Group A)

22. hobby *is* (Problem 1, Situation C)

23. neither carpenter nor cabinet maker *was* (Problem 3, Situation B)

24. both *are* (Problem 2, Group B)

25. economics *are* (Problem 5, Situation B)

26. advisor *plans* (Problem 1, Situation A)

27. team *has* (Problem 4, Situation A)

28. Miss Altheide or nieces *plan* (Problem 3, Situation C)

29. some (students) *are* (Problem 2, Group C)
    some (achievement) *is* (Problem 2, Group C)

30. tractor *needs* (Problem 1, Situation A)

31. lamps *are* (Problem 1, Situation C)

32. either crickets or minnows *make* (Problem 2, Group A)

33. three-fourths (that number of chickens) *are* (Problem 5, Situation E)

34. bull *charges* (Problem 1, Situation B)

35. politics *enters* (Problem 5, Situation B)

36. bills (that number) *bring* (Problem 5, Situation E)

37. cats and a dog *sleep* (Problem 3, Situation A)

38. tree *is* (Problem 1, Situation A)

39. *Sixty Minutes airs* (Problem 5, Situation D)

40. neither desk nor typewriters *belong* (Problem 3, Situation C)

41. data *are* (Problem 5, Situation C)

42. athletics *is* (Problem 5, Situation B)

43. cast *performs* (Problem 4, Situation A)

44. either scrubber or precipitator *is* (Problem 3, Situation B)

45. people *are* (Problem 1, Situation B)

4

PRONOUN USAGE

Often, a writer is not sure about which pronoun to use. Should he say "between you and I" or "between you and me"? Should he say "Us voters are registered" or "We voters are registered"? Should he say "Among those who called are George, Bill, and me" or " . . . George, Bill, and I"?

Ten easy rules should solve all these problems.

RULES

Rule 1: The pronoun-subject of a sentence must be one of these pronouns:

I, you, he, she, it, we, or *they*

Hint:
Usually a writer has no difficulty with this rule unless confused by compound parts.

Example:
Barbara and (he/him) went to the new shopping mall.

To Test:
Use the pronoun alone. Cross out the plural parts:
. . . *he* went to the new shopping mall.

Example:
My sister and (her/she) planned to watch the late show.
. . . *she* planned to watch the late show.

Rule 2: If the pronoun is a predicate word, it must be in the same form as the subject. In other words, after a linking verb, you must use one of the following pronouns:

I, you, he, she, it, we, or *they*

Examples:

It *was I* who called last night.
(I was.)

The man you need to see *is he* in the other room.
(He is.)

The people whom we met *were George and he.*
(George and he were.)

Rule 3: If a pronoun is an object (direct object, indirect object, object of a preposition), use one of these pronouns:

me, you, him, her, it, us, or *them*

Hint 1:
If you have trouble remembering which pronouns are used as objects, say the pronoun with to:

to me, to you, to him, to us, to them

Hint 2:
As in Rule 1, you will probably have no trouble until you meet compound parts.

To Test:
Cross out the compound parts.

Example 1:
The newspaper named Jose and (he/him) as the award recipients.
The newspaper named . . . *him* as the award recipients.
(*Him* is a direct object.)

Example 2:
The carnival man sold (I/me) and (she/her) three tickets.
The carnival man sold *me* . . . three tickets.
(*Me* is an indirect object.)
The carnival man sold . . . *her* three tickets.
(*Her* is an indirect object.)

Example 3:
The Bumbler of the Year Award was given to (he/him) and (I/me).
The Bumbler of the Year Award was given to *him.* . . .
(*Him* is an object of the preposition *to*.)
The Bumbler of the Year Award was given to . . . *me.*
(*Me* is an object of the preposition *to*.)

Rule 4: When a noun immediately follows a pronoun, cross out the noun to make finding the correct pronoun easier.

Example 1:
(We/Us) beekeepers are a rather small group.
We . . . are a rather small group.

Example 2:
The policeman helped (we/us) motorists through the heavily traveled intersection.
The policeman helped *us* . . . through the heavily traveled intersection.

Example 3:
It was (we/us) taxpayers who needed help.
It was *we* . . . who needed help.
(Remember the linking verb here! That is Rule 2.)

Rule 5: When there is a pronoun in a comparison, complete the comparison to help you find the correct pronoun. (You can complete the comparison by adding a verb.)

Example 1:
He is taller than (I/me).
He is taller than *I* [am].

Example 2:
Jeremy works harder than (he/him).
Jeremy works harder than *he* [does].

Example 3:
This young lady is as clever as (he/him).
This young lady is as clever as *he* [is].

Rule 6: Use a possessive pronoun with *-ing* nouns.

Example 1:
We were offended by *his singing.*
(We were not offended by him, only by his singing.)

Example 2:
Mother objected to *my getting* home late.
(Mother did not object to me. She objected to my getting home late. *My* becomes an adjective modifying *getting.*)

Example 3:
His talking caused him constant problems.
(*His* is an adjective modifying *talking.* Possessive pronouns are the only pronouns that can function as adjectives.)

Example 4:
Our frequent *walking* gives me blisters.
(*Our* is an adjective modifying *walking.* It must be a possessive pronoun.)

Rule 7: When a pronoun is used as an appositive, it is in the same form as the word to which it refers. An appositive is a noun that renames another noun preceding it and is set off with commas: *My boss, Mr. Ratherwood, collects Indian relics. Mr. Ratherwood,* the appositive, renames *boss.* If the appositive refers to a subject, you will use the subject form. If the appositive refers to an object, you will use the object form. If the appositive refers to a predicate word, use the subject form.

Example 1:
The two elected to the County Council, Gerry and (he/him), spoke to us.
Gerry and (he/him) is the appositive and refers to the subject, *two.* Since the appositive refers to a subject, you will use the subject form, *he.*

Example 2:
The chairman introduced the evening's two speakers, Dorothea and (I/me).
Dorothea and (I/me) is the appositive and refers to the object *speakers.* Since the appositive refers to an object, you will use the object form, *me.*

Hint:

To make the decision easier, try these two steps:

Step 1:   Cross out the word or words to which the appositive refers.

Step 2:   Read without any compound parts.

Application 1:

Step 1:   The two elected to the County Council, Gerry and (he/him), spoke to us.

               . . . Gerry and (he/him), spoke to us.

Step 2:   . . . (he/him) spoke to us.

Solution: *He* spoke to us.

Application 2:

Step 1:   Martin worked at the sawmill with his two friends, Billy Joe and (he/him).

               Martin worked at the sawmill with . . . Billy Joe and (he/him).

Step 2:   Martin worked at the sawmill with . . . (he/him).

Solution: Martin worked at the sawmill with *him.*

Application 3:

Step 1:   Two neighbors were professional photographers, Mrs. Martin and (he/him).

               Two neighbors were . . . Mrs. Martin and (he/him).

Step 2:   Two neighbors were . . . (he/him).

Solution: Two neighbors were *he* (and Mrs. Martin). (Remember to use the subject form after the linking verb! That is Rule 2 again!)

Rule 8:   Do not use a compound pronoun unless the word it refers to is in the same sentence. The following are compound pronouns:

myself	*herself*	*yourselves*
yourself	*itself*	*themselves*
himself	*ourselves*	

Example 1:

Incorrect: Those who bid on the barnwood picture frames were Mr. Lewis, Miss Qualls, and myself.

Correct: Those who bid on the barnwood picture frames were Mr. Lewis, Miss Qualls, and *I.*

Example 2:

Incorrect: Himself was selected leader.

Correct: He himself was selected leader.

            (Now *himself* refers to *he.*)

Example 3:

Incorrect: Himself bought the antique pocket watch.

Correct: He bought the antique pocket watch *himself.*

            (*Himself* refers to *he.*)

Example 4:
Correct: Mother baked the whole-wheat breads *herself.*
             (*Herself* refers to *Mother.*)

Rule 9:   Use the pronouns *who* and *whom* the same way you would use *he* and *him. Who* is like *he* and *whom* is like *him.* (The *m*'s make remembering easy!)

Hint:
Use these three steps to determine correct use of who *or* whom:
  Step 1:   *Cross out everything up to* who *or* whom.
  Step 2:   *Reword the sentence as necessary.*
  Step 3:   *Substitute* he *or* him *for* who *or* whom.

Application 1:
  Step 1:   We didn't know (who/whom) could operate the new calculator.
              . . . (who/whom) could operate the new calculator.
  Step 2:   (no rewording necessary)
  Step 3:   *He* could operate the new calculator.
  Solution: We didn't know *who* could operate the new calculator.

Application 2:
  Step 1:   I'm not sure (who/whom) you could ask for the money.
              . . . (who/whom) you could ask for the money.
  Step 2:   You could ask (who/whom) for the money.
  Step 3:   You could ask *him* for the money.
  Solution: I'm not sure *whom* you could ask for the money.

Rule 10: Pronouns must agree with the words to which they refer in both number and gender. In other words:

—If the pronoun refers to a singular word, the pronoun must be singular.

—If the pronoun refers to a plural word, the pronoun must be plural.

—If the pronoun refers to a masculine word, the pronoun must be masculine (*he, him, his*).

—If the pronoun refers to a feminine word, the pronoun must be feminine (*she, her, hers*).

—If the pronoun refers to a neuter word, it must be neuter (*it, its, their, theirs, they, them*).

(Obviously, the pronouns *I, we, you,* and *they* in all their forms can be either masculine or feminine.)

Example 1:
Each of the students *was* in *his* seat.
(Did you remember to watch out for that first prepositional phrase? All the other words are singular; the masculine *his* refers to *each.* Since we do not know whether *each* is masculine or feminine—or a combination—we use the masculine form.)

Example 2:

Neither of the boys brought *his* lunch.

(*Neither* is singular [refer to Chapter 3, Problem 2], so the pronoun that refers to it is also singular: *his*.)

Hint:

Four pronouns can cause peculiar problems in agreement:

this, that, these, those

This *and* that *are singular and refer to singular words:* this *sort of* apple, *that* kind of apple. *But* these *and* those *are plural and refer to plural words:* those *kinds of apples,* these *sorts of apples. Never use* them *the way you would use* these *and* those: these *apples, not* them *apples.*

These ten rules for pronoun usage should solve any problems you may have had concerning correct pronoun usage.

REVIEW

Apply these rules now in a review. When you finish, check your answers with those that follow these sentences. Rule numbers are included so that you can review if you find you still have a problem.

Sentences

1. Everyone stood at (his/their) seat when the conductor came into the concert hall.

2. Kenneth is braver than (I/me).

3. (We/Us) secretaries must be able to work with numerous kinds of complicated equipment.

4. (This/These) kinds of apples keep well through winter.

5. The award was given jointly by my brother and (I/me).

6. The two automobile drivers, Mr. Johnston and (he/him), appeared in traffic court yesterday morning.

7. The Boy Scouts try to help (whoever/whomever) is in need.

8. (That/Those) sort of wax bean is especially prolific.

9. All of the students were ready with (his/their) papers.

10. Charles bought my sister and (I/me) some medicinal plants for our greenhouse.

11. Organic gardeners object to (your/you) using nonorganic fertilizers and insecticides.

12. The agricultural agent thought (that/those) kind of shrub would be insect resistant.

13. Race-car drivers must keep (his/their) bodies in excellent condition.

14. The guests who were wearing contact lenses were Carl, Gerald, Tommy, and (she/her).

15. (This/These) kind of print is called a *calico* print.

16. Mathilda and (she/her) prepared homemade hominy.

17. The best model-ship builder in this community is (he/him) in the red plaid shirt.

18. The chirping crickets lulled (he/him) and (I/me) to sleep.

19. (He/Himself) collected moths as a hobby.

20. Mother said that each child had to pick up (his/their) own toys.

21. The nominees for president and vice-president will probably be Mrs. Gallmeister and (I/me) respectively.

22. Shoveling snow in sub-zero weather delighted neither (he/him) nor (I/me).

23. United Parcel Service delivered a package addressed to (we/us) boys in the family.

24. Several students made better grades than (he/him).

25. The nighthawk objected to (me/my) being near her eggs, which were lying in the gravel of the courtyard.

26. Someone left (his/their) jacket lying on the bench.

27. The barometer was won by a man (who/whom) the neighbors said would enjoy using it.

28. Daddy bought a new compact car for (him/himself).

29. The naturalist and (she/her) led our group along a fascinating nature trail.

30. The motorcycle riders selected two riders they themselves thought excellent, Robert and (he/him).

31. Did everybody get all the cake and ice cream (he/they) wanted?

32. The best bread-baker in Vanderburgh County was (she/her).

33. The man (who/whom) they selected to be the speaker was pleased to accept the invitation.

34. Each of the members cast (his/their) ballots for the four officers.

35. The valedictorian will be (he or she/him or her) who has the highest grade-point average.

Solutions

1. his (Rule 10): *Everyone* is singular.

2. I [am] (Rule 5)

3. We (Rule 4)

4. These (Rule 10)

5. me (Rule 3): *By* is a preposition and needs an object.

6. he (Rule 7): *He* renames part of the subject, *drivers*.

7. whoever (Rule 9): Think "*he* is in need."

8. That (Rule 10)

9. their (Rule 10)

10. me (Rule 3): Charles bought *me* plants.

11. your (Rule 6)

12. that (Rule 10)

13. their (Rule 10)

14. she (Rule 2): The linking verb *were* requires the same form as the subject: *she*.

15. This (Rule 10)

16. she (Rule 1):   Think "she prepared."

17. he (Rule 2):   The linking verb *is* requires the same form as the subject.

18. him and me (Rule 3)

19. He (Rule 8)

20. his (Rule 10):   *Each child* is singular and so requires a singular pronoun.

21. I (Rule 2):   The linking verb *will be* requires the same form as the subject.

22. him nor me (Rule 3)

23. us (Rule 4)

24. he [did] (Rule 5)

25. my (Rule 6)

26. his (Rule 10):   *Someone* is singular and so requires a singular pronoun.

27. who (Rule 9):   Think "the neighbors said *he* would enjoy using it."

28. himself (Rule 8)

29. she (Rule 1)

30. him (Rule 7):   Think "the riders selected *him.*"

31. he (Rule 10):   *Everybody* is singular and so requires a singular pronoun.

32. she (Rule 2):   Here is another linking verb!

33. whom (Rule 9):   Think "they selected *him.*"

34. his (Rule 10):   *Each* is singular and so requires a singular pronoun. Do not let the prepositional phrase *of the members* interfere.

35. he or she (Rule 2):   It is another linking verb!

5

ADJECTIVE AND ADVERB USAGE

Another usage problem occurs when speakers and writers must decide whether to use an adjective form or an adverb form. Should you say, "I don't feel good," "I don't feel well," "I feel bad," or "I feel badly"?

In order to help solve any problems you may have with adjective and adverb usage, remember these two principles from Chapter 1:

1. Adjectives must modify *nouns.*
2. Adverbs must modify *verbs, adjectives,* or other *adverbs.*

Some basic rules will help you solve other problems you may have with adjectives and adverbs:

RULES

Rule 1: Use adverbs to modify action verbs.

Example:
Harold drives his new car *carefully.*
(*Carefully,* an adverb, modifies the action verb *drives.*)

Rule 2: Use adverbs to modify adjectives.

Example:
We thought the test was *really* (not *real*) difficult.
(*Really,* an adverb, modifies the adjective *difficult.*)

Rule 3: Use an adjective after a linking verb. (Remember, substitute some form of *to be* to test for a linking verb.)

Example 1:
The owner of the automobile appeared *angry.*
(*Appeared* is a linking verb: *The owner of the automobile is angry.* So we need the adjective *angry.*)

Example 2:
The owner of the car appeared *suddenly.*
(Now *appeared* is an action verb. You cannot say, *The owner of the*

car is suddenly. So, since *appeared* is an action verb, you must use the adverb *suddenly.* See Rule 1.)

Rule 4:   *Bad* is an adjective; *badly* is an adverb. Use the adjective, *bad,* after a linking verb.

Example 1:
He feels *bad.*
(*Feels* is a linking verb and so requires the adjective *bad.*)

Example 2:
The repairman did a *bad* job on the car.
(*Bad* functions as an adjective to modify the noun *job.*)

Example 3:
The inexperienced actor performed *badly* even in the small role.
(*Badly* functions as an adverb to modify the verb *performed.*)

Rule 5:   *Good* is an adjective; *well* can be an adjective *or* an adverb.

When *well* is an adjective, it means

a. in good health

b. of good appearance

c. satisfactory

Note:
Usually, *well* as an adjective is used after a linking verb.

Example 1:
Charlie did a *good* job welding the lawnmower handle back in place.
(*Good* is an adjective modifying the noun *job.*)

Example 2:
Mother looks *well* in that dress.
(*Well* here is an adjective meaning "of good appearance" after a linking verb, *looks.*)

Example 3:
He did the job *well.*
(*Well* is now used as an adverb modifying the action verb *did.*)

Example 4:
All is *well.*
(*Well* is an adjective meaning "satisfactory" after the linking verb *is.*)

Example 5:
I don't fell *well.*
(*Well* is an adjective meaning "in good health" after the linking verb *do feel.*)

Rule 6:   Use *fewer* to refer to countable things and *less* to refer to amounts.

Example 1:
The recipe calls for *less* sugar than vinegar.
(You cannot count sugar: one sugar, two sugars.)

Example 2:
My recipe calls for *fewer* cups of sugar than yours does.
(You *can* count cups of sugar: one cup of sugar, two cups of sugar.)

Example 3:
Bob has *less* money than Gino.
(You *cannot* count money: one money, two monies.)

Example 4:
Bob has fewer dollar bills than Gino.
(You *can* count dollar bills: one dollar-bill, two dollar-bills.)

Hint:
Anytime you use fewer *or* less, *be sure to say fewer or less* than what.

Example:
Incorrect: The oak tree has fewer leaves.
Correct: The oak tree has fewer leaves *than the maple tree.*

Rule 7: Distinguish between the comparative and the superlative forms.
Part A.   If you are discussing *two* things, use the comparative form of the adjective or adverb. (The comparative form ends in *-er* or uses the word *more.*)

Example 1:
Paul is the *older* one of the two brothers.

Example 2:
Jed is the *taller* one of the two men.

Example 3:
Tex is the *more handsome* of the two actors.

Part B.   If you are discussing more than two, use the superlative form. (The superlative form ends in *-est* or uses the word *most.*)

Example 1:
Aunt Mary is the *tallest* one of the three sisters.

Example 2:
Katherine is the *most energetic* of the group.

Rule 8: Avoid double negatives.

Example 1:
Incorrect: We did*n't* do *no* homework.
Correct: We didn't do any homework.

Example 2:
Incorrect: There are*n't hardly* any good building sites left there anymore.
Correct: There are hardly any good building sites left there anymore.

Rule 9:   Avoid illogical comparisons.

Example:
Illogical: Quincy is taller than any student in his class.
(But since Quincy is, obviously, in his own class, you are
saying that he is taller than himself!)
Better: Quincy is taller than any *other* student in his class.

These nine rules, when applied correctly, should keep you out of trouble with
adjective and adverb usage. Check, now, to see if you understand.

REVIEW

Check yourself on the review below. If you miss an item, be sure to go back to the rule and study the examples for further clarification. Rule numbers are given with the answers following these sentences.

Sentences

1. The medicated lotion was (good/well) for bee stings.

2. Marjorie felt (bad/badly) about having embarrassed her dear friend.

3. The mongrel appeared (happy/happily) lying there on the velvet cushion.

4. When in training, our neighbor runs four miles a day (regular/regularly).

5. Lately, our winters have been (real/really) cold.

6. The leg was broken (bad/badly).

7. Compared with my brother, I am the (taller/tallest) one.

8. I have little patience, but she has even (fewer/less).

9. The caterers (didn't hardly have/hardly had) enough food for everyone.

10. Clovis won more awards than (anyone/anyone else) in his sales district.

11. The vice-president of the group is the (more/most) assertive of the officers.

12. There are (fewer/less) cars in the parking lot now than there were at noon.

13. After being sick yesterday, Father says he is feeling (good/well) today.

14. The situation appeared (bad/badly).

15. The holiday was a (delightful/delightfully) beautiful day.

16. The colors in the five-piece outfit went together (good/well).

17. There are three of us girls in the family, and Sue Ellen is the (older/oldest) one of my sisters.

18. The child behaved (bad/badly).

19. The job was done (good/well).

20. Marilyn looks (good/well) with her hair cut short.

Solutions

1. good (Rule 5)

2. bad (Rule 4): *Felt* is a linking verb.

3. happy (Rule 3): *Appeared* is a linking verb.

4. regularly (Rule 1)

5. really (Rule 2): *Really,* the adverb, is required to modify the predicate adjective *cold.*

6. badly (Rule 4): *Badly* modifies the action verb *was broken.*

7. taller (Rule 7)

8. less (Rule 6)

9. hardly had (Rule 8)

10. anyone else (Rule 9)

11. most (Rule 7)

12. fewer (Rule 6)

13. well (Rule 5): The adjective *well* is used here to mean "in good health."

14. bad (Rule 4): *Appeared* is a linking verb.

15. delightfully (Rule 2)

16. well (Rule 5): *Well* is used an adverb to modify the action verb *went.*

17. older (Rule 7): Bet you goofed! If there are three of us, then I have only two sisters.

18. badly (Rule 4): *Badly* modifies the action verb *behaved.*

19. well (Rule 5): The adverb modifies the action verb *was done.*

20. well (Rule 5): The adjective means "of good appearance."

6

TROUBLESOME VERBS

Irregular verbs often create problems. Your dictionary will solve most of these problems. Three pairs of verbs, however, create special problems because the verbs in each pair look so much alike:

Present	Past	Participle (Test with *has, have,* or *had)*	Progressive
sit	sat	sat	sitting
set	set	set	setting
rise	rose	risen	rising
raise	raised	raised	raising
lie	lay	lain	lying
lay	laid	laid	laying

SPECIAL PROBLEM - VERBS

Pair 1: Sit/Set

Sit means "to rest," as in a chair.
Set means "to put or place."

Examples:
The team members will *sit* together.
The team members will *set* their goals.

Note:
Sit will not take a direct object. *Set must* have a direct object, either stated or implied. So anytime you use the word *set,* there must be an answer to the question, "Set *who* or *what*?"

Pair 2: Rise/Raise

Rise, like *sit,* will not take a direct object.
Raise, like *set,* must have a direct object.

Example 1:
The window *rises* mysteriously.
(no direct object)

71

Example 2:
Please *raise* the windows!
Ask, "Raise *who* or *what*?" Answer: *windows*

Example 3:
The bread dough *rose* almost double in an hour.
(no direct object)

Example 4:
That truck farmer *raises* especially beautiful produce.
Ask, "Raises *who* or *what*?" Answer: *produce.*

Pair 3:   Lie/Lay

Lie means to rest or recline, and, like *rise* and *sit,* will not take a direct object.

Lay means to put or place, and, like *raise* and *set,* it *must* have a direct object.

What makes these two verbs so confusing is that *lay* in the present is the same as *lie* in the past:

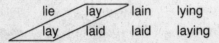

Hint:
To help you select the correct word, test by substituting "rest or recline" for the forms of lie *and "put or place" for the forms of* lay.

Example 1:
(Lie/Lay) the baby in her crib.
Substitute: Put or place the baby in her crib.
Solution: *Lay* the baby in her crib.

Example 2:
(Laying/Lying) in the sun can cause unfortunate side effects.
Substitute: Resting or reclining in the sun can cause unfortunate side effects.
Solution: *Lying* in the sun can cause unfortunate side effects.

Summary

$$
\left.\begin{array}{l}
s(i)t \\
r(i)se \\
l(i)e
\end{array}\right\} \text{ have } no \text{ direct objects}
$$

(Think of *i* as representing *i*ndependent: not dependent on a direct object for existence!)

$$
\left.\begin{array}{l}
set \\
raise \\
lay
\end{array}\right\} \ must \text{ have direct objects}
$$

REVIEW

Check your understanding of these three pairs of verbs by working through the following sentences. When you finish, check your answers with those that follow these sentences.

Sentences

1. When I finish raking the lawn, I plan to (lay/lie) down for a nap.

2. Grandpa always (set/sat) in a high-backed wicker rocker.

3. The temperature and our tempers were both (raising/rising).

4. "He can't come to the phone," she explained; "he's just (laid/lain) down."

5. The gardener was (sitting/setting) tomato plants in three one-hundred-foot rows.

6. The family pet, a dog of mixed descent, (lay/laid) in front of the television set.

7. (Lying/Laying) flat on his back, the football player appeared to be injured.

8. The group did exercises in a (sitting/setting) position.

9. The doctor's report (raised/rose) the family's hopes.

10. Those old newspapers have (lain/laid) there for three weeks now.

11. Citizens watched in helpless frustration as the flood waters (raised/rose).

12. Please (sit/set) the baby in this chair, not that one.

13. The big Persian cat, (laying/lying) in the open window, dozed peacefully.

14. Come and (set/sit) with us!

15. The toys were (laying/lying) along the edge of the driveway.

Solutions

1. lie (no direct object; substitute *rest*)

2. sat (no direct object)

3. rising (no direct object)

4. lain (no direct object; substitute *reclined*)

5. setting (direct object: plants)

6. lay (no direct object; substitute *rested*)

7. Lying (no direct object; substitute *reclining*)

8. sitting (no direct object)

9. raised (direct object: hopes)

10. lain (no direct object; substitute *reclined*)

11. rose (no direct object)

12. set (direct object: baby)

13. lying (no direct object; substitute *resting*)

14. sit (no direct object)

15. lying (no direct object; substitute *reclining*)

III

PHRASES AND CLAUSES

7

VERBALS

You can get through life quite comfortably without knowing anything about verbals. In fact, verbals function as nouns, adjectives, or adverbs; so, in essence, you already know about them from Chapter 1. Why, then, spend any time talking about them? For the purposes of this book, there is one primary reason: understanding some of the basics about verbals will make understanding punctuation much easier. For the purposes of improving your writing, there is a secondary reason. Knowing how to use verbals will improve your ability to vary sentence structure. (There were three verbals in that last sentence, by the way!)

Verbals are words that look like verbs but are not used as verbs. Verbals can be used as nouns, adjectives, or adverbs; so they can function in the following ways:

subjects

direct objects

objects of prepositions

predicate words

appositives

noun modifiers

verb modifiers

adjective modifiers

adverb modifiers

We will talk about the characteristics and functions of the three kinds of verbals:

infinitives

gerunds

participles

PART I: INFINITIVES

A. **Characteristics:** An infinitive has the following characteristics to help you recognize it:

1. Basic appearance: An infinitive is made up of *to* plus a verb.

    Example 1:
    To sing is his goal.
    (*To* plus the verb *sing* makes the infinitive.)

    Example 2:
    He wanted *to work* late.
    (*To* and the verb *work* make the infinitive.)

2. Infinitive phrase: Verbals, like verbs, take both adverb modifiers
    and direct objects. The infinitive and its objects and/or modifiers
    form the infinitive phrase. (Remember that objects answer *who?* or
    what? after the verbal; adverb modifiers tell *how, when, where,* or *to
    what extent.*)

    Example:
    He wanted *to drive the borrowed car carefully.*
    (*To* and the verb *drive* make the infinitive. If you ask, "To drive *who*
    or *what?*," you get *car* as your answer. That, of course, is the object
    of the infinitive *to drive. Carefully* tells *how* about the infinitive *to
    drive,* so it is an adverb modifier. The entire infinitive phrase, then, is
    to drive the borrowed car carefully.

    To put it simply:

    $$to + verb + \left\{ \begin{array}{l} \text{object(s)} \\ \text{and/or} \\ \text{modifier(s)} \end{array} \right\} = \text{infinitive phrase}$$

    Now consider this additional example:

    Example:
    To instruct his young relatives in the routines of square dancing was
    the fiddler's only desire.
    Infinitive: *to instruct* (*to* + the verb *instruct*)
    Object: *relatives* (Instruct *who* or *what?*)
    Modifiers: *young* (adjective modifying the object *relatives*); *in the
                 routines* (prepositional phrase that modifies *instruct*);
                 and *of square dancing* (prepositional phrase that modi-
                 fies *routines*)
    The entire infinitive phrase, then, is *to instruct his young relatives in
    the routines of square dancing.*

    Warning:
    Remember that not every *to* will introduce an infinitive.

    > *to* + noun = prepositional phrase
    > *to* + verb = infinitive

    Example 1:
    He walked to the concert hall early.
    (*To the concert hall* is *to* plus the noun *hall* and so is a preposi-
    tional phrase, not an infinitive.)

    Example 2:
    He walked to keep trim.
    (*To keep trim* is *to* plus the verb *keep* and, therefore, an infinitive.

B. **Function:** An infinitive or infinitive phrase functions as a noun or as an adjective or as an adverb. Think of the whole phrase as *one word.* You can then use the sentence-attack plan to determine which part of the sentence it is. (See Chapter 2.) If the infinitive does not fit in the sentence-attack plan, then you know you have a modifier.

Consider now the specific functions of an infinitive:

1. Noun: Since an infinitive functions as a noun, it can function in most of the ways a noun can function:

   a. As subject

      Example:
      To become educated was their primary ambition.
      (*To become educated* is the subject of *was.*)

   b. As predicate word

      Example:
      The program's purpose was *to entertain.*
      (*To entertain* follows the linking verb *was* and renames the subject *purpose.*)

   c. As an appositive

      Example:
      While in college, Marlene had only one goal: *to get as thorough an education as possible.*
      (Remember that an appositive renames a noun. *To get as thorough an education as possible* renames *goal.*)

   d. As direct object

      Example:
      The City Councilman wanted *to expand the Park Board budget.*
      (*To expand the Park Board budget* answers *what?* after the action verb *wanted.*)

2. Adjective: As an adjective, an infinitive modifies a noun:

   Example:
   This is the class *to take!*
   (*To take* modifies the noun *class.*)

3. Adverb: Like other adverbs, infinitives can modify verbs, adjectives, and other adverbs:

   a. As verb modifier

      Example:
      Martha has gone *to visit her sister in New Orleans.*
      (*To visit her sister in New Orleans* answers the adverb question *where?* about the action verb *gone.*)

   b. As adjective modifier

      Example:
      You were lucky *to pass the course.*

(*To pass the course* explains *how* about the predicate adjective *lucky*.)

    c. As adverb modifier

Example:
The doctor operated too late *to save the accident victim.*
(*To save the accident victim* explains *to what extent* about the adverb *late*.)

C. "To-less" infinitive: Sometimes the infinitive appears without the word *to*.

Example:
May I help you bake the cookies?
(*Bake the cookies,* a "*to*-less" infinitive, is the direct object of *help*.)

D. Process: Use the following steps to identify the function of the infinitive phrase:

Step 1: Identify the phrase.
Step 2: Think of the phrase as one word.
Step 3: Use the sentence-attack plan to determine the functions of subject, direct object and predicate word.
Step 4: If the phrase does not fit in the sentence-attack plan, you will know the phrase is a modifier.

Example 1:
The incumbent hoped to win the election.
Step 1: The incumbent hoped *to win the election.*
Step 2: Think: The incumbent hoped towintheelection.
Step 3: a. Find the verb: *hoped*
          b. *Hoped* is an action verb.
          c. Ask: *who* or *what* hoped?
              Answer: *incumbent* (subject)
          d. Ask: incumbent hoped *who* or *what?*
              Answer: *towintheelection*
              (The infinitive phrase is the direct object.)

Example 2:
The man to see about gardening problems is the county agent.
Step 1: The man *to see about gardening problems* is the county agent.
Step 2: Think: The man toseeaboutgardeningproblems is the county agent.
Step 3: a. Find the verb: *is*
          b. *Is* is a linking verb.
          c. Ask: *who* or *what is?*
              Answer: *man* (subject)
          d. Ask: man is *who* or *what?*
              Answer: *agent* (predicate noun)
Step 4: The infinitive did not fit in the sentence-attack plan, so it must be a modifier. *To see about gardening problems* answers

which one about the noun *man,* so the infinitive phrase functions as an adjective.

E. **Usage:** As you begin consciously using infinitive phrases to increase sentence variety, keep in mind that the *to* and the verb form should not be separated:

Example:
Incorrect: He planned *to* not *go* on a vacation this year.
Correct: He planned not *to go* on a vacation this year.

The separation of *to* from the verb form is called a *split infinitive.* Effective writers and speakers try to avoid split infinitives.

PART II: GERUNDS

A. **Characteristics:** A gerund has the following characteristics to help you recognize it:

1. Basic appearance: A gerund ends in *-ing.*

    Example 1:
    Swimming at Hartke Pool is his favorite pastime.

    Example 2:
    Running weekend marathons in the city keeps him in good physical shape.

    Example 3:
    He considered *running* for office.

    Example 4:
    After *eating* the cake and ice cream, I felt stuffed.

2. Gerund phrases: Gerunds, like infinitives, can take objects and modifiers. All of these together make up the gerund phrase:

    > *-ing* word
    > +
    > object(s)   } = gerund phrase
    > +
    > modifier(s)

    Example 1:
    Swimming at Hartke Pool is his favorite pastime.
    (*At Hartke Pool* modifies *swimming* by explaining *where.* So the entire gerund phrase is the gerund plus its modifier: *swimming at Hartke Pool.*)

    Example 2:
    Running weekend marathons in the city keeps him in good physical shape.
    (*Marathons* answers *what?* about *running,* so it is the object of the gerund. *Weekend* describes *which* about *marathons. In the city,* a

prepositional phrase, functions as an adverb to tell *where* about *marathons*. The gerund and its object and modifiers, then, make up the entire gerund phrase: *running weekend marathons in the city*.)

Example 3:
He considered *running for office.*
(*For office* tells *how?* about *running,* so the gerund phrase is *running for office.*)

Example 4:
After *eating the cake and ice cream,* I felt stuffed.
(*Cake and ice cream* answer *what?* after *eating* and are the compound objects of the gerund. They and the gerund make up the complete gerund phrase: *eating the cake and ice cream.*)

Warning:
Not all *-ing* words are gerunds. With that warning in mind, think about *function.*

B. **Function:**   A gerund or a gerund phrase functions as a noun. (Remember, think of the phrase as a single word.)

1. As subject

    Example:
    Playing flag football was not his idea of fun.
    (*Playing flag football* is the subject of *was.*)

2. As predicate word

    Example:
    Aunt Mary's hobby is *crocheting doilies.*
    (*Crocheting doilies* answers *what?* after the linking verb *is* and renames the subject *hobby.*)

3. As direct object

    Example:
    Most people enjoy *listening to music.*
    (*Listening to music* answers *what?* after the action verb *enjoy.*)

4. As object of the preposition

    Example:
    The attorney won the case by *proving the witness a liar.*
    (*By* is a preposition, and *proving the witness a liar* answers *by what?* The whole prepositional phrase functions to tell *how?* about the verb *won.*)

5. As appositive

    Example:
    His job, *collecting data for the Environmental Protection Agency,* required painstaking effort.
    (Remember, an appositive, which renames another noun, is usually

set off with commas. This gerund phrase, which functions as an appositive, renames the noun *job*.)

Now let us reconsider the Warning:

Not all *-ing* words are gerunds. Which of the following *-ing* words are gerunds?

1. Robert is *swimming* forty laps a day, now.

2. The small child, *walking* alone, became lost.

3. *Sobbing,* the old woman sank to her knees.

4. Woolen garments are *rising* in price.

5. The puppy was *chewing* on my shoes for two days.

None of these *-ing* words are gerunds. Why? None of them function as *nouns*. Look at the following explanations:

1. *Is swimming* is the verb.

2. *Walking* functions as an adjective.

3. *Sobbing* functions as an adjective.

4. *Are rising* is the verb.

5. *Was chewing* is the verb.

Remember:
Function tells all. To be gerunds, *-ing* words must function as *nouns*.

PART III: PARTICIPLES

A. **Characteristics:** Participles have the following characteristics to help you recognize them:

1. Basic appearance: Because there are two kinds of participles, they have two different forms:

    a. Past participles usually end in *-ed* (the form of the verb you would use with the helping words *have* or *has:* have *walked*, have *taken*, have *sung*.)

        Example:
        The picture frame, *mottled* with old paint, needed refinishing.

    b. Present participles end in *-ing*. (So they *look* like gerunds. They do *not*, however, function as gerunds do.)

        Example:
        The picture *hanging* above the sofa depicts a pastoral scene.

2. Participial phrases: Just like infinitives and gerunds, participles can have objects and modifiers.

$$\left.\begin{array}{c} \text{participle} \\ + \\ \text{object(s)} \\ + \\ \text{modifiers(s)} \end{array}\right\} = \text{participial phrase}$$

a. As present participial phrase

Example 1:
Walking home from school, John tripped on the sidewalk.
(*Home* tells *where* about *walking;* and *from school,* a prepositional phrase, modifies *walking.* The whole phrase, then, is the participle plus its modifiers: *walking home from school.*)

Example 2:
Singing a haunting melody, the soloist won the audience's approval.
(*Melody* answers *what?* about *singing,* so it is the object of the participle. *Haunting* tells *what kind* about *melody.* So the whole participial phrase is *singing a haunting melody.*)

b. As past participial phrase

Example:
Beaten by the wind, the tomato plants looked wilted.
(*By the wind* tells *how* about *beaten;* then the whole participial phrase is made of the participle and its modifier: *beaten by the wind.*)

B. **Function:** Participles always function as adjectives. They modify nouns. As adjectives, participles may serve in the following ways:

1. Noun modifier

Example 1:
Walking down the road, we saw a fox terrier.
(The participle modifies the subject *we.*)

Example 2:
We saw a fox terrier *walking down the road.*
(The participle modifies the object *terrier.*)

2. Predicate word

Example 1:
The supervisor was *mistaken.*
(*Mistaken* follows the linking verb *was* and describes the subject *supervisor.*)

Example 2:
The defendant seemed *unconcerned about the attorney's questioning.*
(The participial phrase follows the linking verb *seemed* and describes the subject *defendant.*)

C. **Usage:** When the participial phrase appears at the beginning of a sentence, the phrase is followed by a comma. The phrase will modify the noun immediately after the comma. (You will learn other punctuation rules for participial phrases in Chapter 9.)

Example:
Watching the sunrise from inside their tent, the two campers reveled in their enjoyment of the peace and quiet.
(The participial phrase, followed by a comma, modifies *campers,* the first noun after the comma.)

Warning:
Since the participial phrase *must* modify the first noun after the comma, be sure to avoid ridiculous sentences:

Example 1:
Ridiculous: Arriving late at the bus stop, the bus went off without me.
(The *bus* did not arrive late!)
Better: Arriving late at the bus stop, I missed the bus.
(The participial phrase must modify the noun after the comma: *I.*)

Example 2:
Ridiculous: Having forgotten to wind it, the clock stopped at midnight.
(The *clock* did not forget to wind itself!)
Better: Having forgotten to wind the clock, I found it had stopped at midnight.

Example 3:
Ridiculous: Walking home from the graveyard, an old abandoned house seemed especially eerie.
(A *house* walking??)
Better: Walking home from the graveyard, Robert thought the old abandoned house seemed especially eerie.

REVIEW

Look at the following sentences and find the verbals. Identify the kind of verbal (infinitive, gerund, or participle) and its function (subject, modifier of noun, predicate word, etc.). Answers appear following the sentences. See if you really understand. Hint: *Some sentences have more than one verbal.*

Sentences

1. Startled, he stood quietly, breathing rapidly.

2. An excellent form of exercise is jogging at a steady, even pace for a mile or so.

3. To find the old cemetery, we followed the nearly invisible trail; but, suffering from the heat, we gave up.

4. To eat moderately seemed advisable.

5. Washing a car is sometimes tedious to do.

6. The old man's hobby was playing in a German folk band.

7. After the heavy snows ceased, I no longer wished to be confined to the house.

8. The try-outs, conducted by the orchestra director and her assistant, were held once each year.

9. Sustained by chocolate, I shall win all battles except those with the waist-line.

10. Having refused his phone call, Evelyn had little chance of accepting his apology.

Solutions

1. *Startled* is a participle and functions as an adjective to modify the noun *he*. *Breathing rapidly* is a participial phrase and functions to modify the noun *he*. (Remember, participles can modify only *nouns,* not verbs.)

2. *Jogging at a steady, even pace for a mile or so* is a gerund phrase and is the predicate word after the linking verb *is*.

3. *To find the old cemetery* is an infinitive phrase and functions as an adverb to modify the verb *followed*. *Suffering from the heat* is a participial phrase and functions as an adjective to modify the noun *we*.

4. *To eat moderately* is an infinitive phrase and is the subject of the sentence.

5. *Washing a car* is a gerund phrase and is the subject of the sentence. *To do* is an infinitive and functions as an adverb to modify the adjective *tedious*.

6. *Playing in a German folk band* is a gerund phrase and is the predicate word after the linking verb *was*.

7. *To be confined to the house* is an infinitive phrase; and, in a noun function, it is the direct object of the verb *wished*.

8. *Conducted by the orchestra director and her assistant* is a participial phrase and functions as an adjective to modify the noun *try-outs*.

9. *Sustained by chocolate* is a participial phrase and functions as an adjective to modify the noun *I*.

10. *Having refused his phone call* is a participial phrase and functions as an adjective to modify the noun *Evelyn*. *Accepting his apology* is a gerund phrase; and, acting as a noun, it is the object of the preposition *of*.

8

CLAUSES

There are two kinds of clauses:

1. main clauses (sometimes called *independent* clauses) with subjects and verbs that can stand alone as sentences

2. subordinate clauses (sometimes called *dependent* clauses), which have subjects and verbs but cannot stand alone.

    Examples:

    . . . after the *snow began*. . . .

    . . . *that stands* in the front yard. . . .

    . . . that *I told* you about. . . .

Notice that clauses are different from phrases in that clauses *must* have subjects and verbs; phrases do not have subjects and verbs.

There are three kinds of subordinate clauses that we will be studying in this chapter:

noun clause

adjective clause

adverb clause

PART I: NOUN CLAUSE

A. Characteristics:

1. The noun clause will have a subject and a verb and will usually start with one of these words:

who	which
whose	what
whom	that

    (*Ever* can be added to most of these words, too: *whoever, whatever.*)

    Example 1:
    That man is *who came to the door.*
    (Subject, *who;* verb, *came*)

Example 2:
No one knew *whose book was left behind.*
(Subject, *book;* verb, *was left*)

Example 3:
I talked with *whomever the company sent to settle my claim.*
(Subject, *company;* verb, *sent*)

Example 4:
Which party is guilty is the question.
(Subject, *party;* verb, *is*)

Example 5:
There is no excuse for *what happened.*
(Subject, *what;* verb, *happened*)

Example 6:
Brad explained *that Jim's work was done exceptionally well.*
(Subject, *work;* verb, *was done*)

2. Sometimes the first word in the noun clause is the subject of the verb of the clause.

    Example:
    . . . who came to the door. . . .
    (*Who* is the subject of the verb *came.*)

3. The clause may have an object and/or modifiers.

    Example 1:
    . . . who came *to the door.* . . .
    (*To the door,* a prepositional phrase, tells *where* about *came,* so the phrase is an adverb modifier.)

    Example 2:
    Whoever designed the building took credit for its striking appearance.
    (*Building* answers *what?* after the action verb *designed,* so it is the direct object of *designed.*)

4. Sometimes, the first word in the noun clause is the object of the verb or a predicate word.

    Example 1:
    What he saw startled him.
    (*He* is the subject of the action verb *saw; what* is the direct object of *saw.*)

    Example 2:
    No one knew *who she was.*
    (*Who* is the predicate word after the linking verb *was.*)

B. **Function:** The noun clause may function many of the same ways a single noun functions:

    1. As subject

Example:
Whoever called you yesterday mispronounced your name.
(The noun clause, when thought of as a single word, answers *who?* in front of the verb.)

2. As predicate word

    Example:
    His faith is *what keeps him alive.*
    (The noun clause follows the linking verb *is* and renames *faith.* Notice that the sentence order can be reversed so that the noun clause becomes the subject: *What keeps him alive* is his faith.)

3. As direct object

    Example:
    The witness explained *what he saw.*
    (The noun clause answers *what?* after the action verb *explained.*)

4. As object of preposition

    Example:
    Unfortunately, people are sometimes judged by *what they wear.*
    (*By* is a preposition, and the noun clause, when thought of as a single word, answers the question *by what?*)

5. As appositive

    Example:
    My long-range concern, *that you learn grammar,* helps me to keep finding examples!
    (The noun clause renames the noun *concern* and is set off with commas.)

C. **Attack plan:** Use the following steps to determine the function of the noun clause.

    Step 1: Find the clause, beginning with one of the special words (*who, whose, whom, which, what,* or *that*) and ending after all the modifiers and/or objects.
    Step 2: Think of the clause as a single word.
    Step 3: Use the sentence-attack plan (see Chapter 2) to determine how the noun is used. (An appositive will rename, remember, and so will not fit in the sentence-attack plan.)

Example:
What happens next remains to be seen.
Step 1: Find the clause: *what happens next* (*What* is the subject of the verb *happens; next* tells *when* about *happens.*)
Step 2: Think of the clause as one word:
         Whathappensnext remains to be seen.
Step 3: Use the sentence-attack plan:
         a. Find the verb: *remains*

b. *Remains* is a linking verb. (You can
substitute *is,* a form of *to be.*)

c. *Who* or *what* remains?
Answer: *whathappensnext*

So, the noun clause is the *subject* of the sentence.

PART II: ADJECTIVE CLAUSE

A. **Characteristics:** The adjective clause will have a subject and a verb
and will usually start with one of these words:

who	whose	whom
which	that	

Sometimes, *when* and *where* can introduce adjective clauses.

Example 1:
The athlete *who won the Best Sportsmanship Award* was captain of her
basketball team.
(Subject, *who;* verb, *won*)

Example 2:
The lucky person *whose name is drawn* will win a three-day vacation in
Miami.
(Subject, *name;* verb, *is drawn*)

Example 3:
The sidewalk artist could draw a caricature of any famous person *whom
you could name.*
(Subject, *you;* verb, *could name*)

Example 4:
My brother ate all the strawberries *that I picked.*
(Subject, *I;* verb, *picked*)

Example 5:
We reminisced about the time *when we celebrated our graduation from
high school.*
(Subject, *we;* verb, *celebrated*)

Example 6:
This is the place *where the accident happened.*
(Subject, *accident;* verb, *happened*)

B. **Function:** The adjective clause functions the same way a single adjective functions: it answers *which one? what kind?* or *how many?* about a
noun.

Example:
The flower arrangement *that was judged Best of Show* was made up of
dried cornshuck flowers.
(*That was judged Best of Show* says *which* about *arrangement;* the
clause functions as an adjective modifying the noun *arrangment.*)

C.   **Attack plan:**   Since the adjective clause and the noun clause can begin with many of the same words, you will need to consider *function* in order to know whether the clause is an adjective or noun clause.

Remember:

If you use the sentence-attack plan, the *noun* clause will fit into the plan at some point (with the single exception of the appositive). So, if you finish all steps in the sentence-attack plan and have found no use for the clause, you can be fairly certain that the clause is a *modifier.*

Example:

The boy *whose jacket is lying on the ground* is playing tennis in the second court.

(*Jacket* is the subject of *is lying; on the ground* is a prepositional phrase that tells *where* about *is lying; whose* is possessive and modifies *jacket.*)

Sentence-attack plan:

Step 1:   Cross out *in the second court* (prepositional phrase).

Step 2:   *Is playing* is the action verb.

Step 3:   *Who* or *what* is playing?
              Answer: *boy* (subject)

Step 4:   Boy is playing *who* or *what?*
              Answer: *tennis* (direct object)

Step 5:   Boy is playing tennis *to whom* or *for whom?*
              Answer: none

So what remains is a modifier. Remember that you must think of the clause as if it were one word. *Whosejacketislyingontheground* tells *which* about the noun *boy;* so the clause is an adjective.

Warning:

Sometimes the clue word (especially the word *that*) is not included:

> *Example:*
> Here is the house *I told you about.*
> ([*That*] *I told you about* is the adjective clause.)

Hint 1:

People sometimes confuse <u>who</u>, <u>which</u>, and <u>that</u>.

   a.   *Who* (or *whom* or *whose*) refers to people.

        Example:
        He is the politican *who* made all those promises.

   b.   *Which* refers to things or non-human animals.

        Example 1:
        This tree, *which* stands taller than any others nearby, provides shade for both of our yards.
        (*Which* refers to the thing *tree.*)

        Example 2:
        Our neighbor owns an AKC-registered dog, *which* howls during the early morning hours.
        (*Which* refers to the non-human animal *dog.*)

   c.   *That* also refers to things or non-human animals, but it should not be used when the adjective clause is set off with commas.

Example 1:
This tree, *which* [not *that*] stands taller than any others nearby, provides shade for both of our yards.

Example 2:
Our neighbor owns the dog *that* howls during the early morning hours.

Hint 2:
Do not use <u>what</u> *to start an adjective clause.*

Example:
Incorrect: The car *what* is painted blue is my mother's car.
Correct: The car *that* is painted blue is my mother's car.
Correct: The car, *which* is painted blue, is my mother's.

Hint 3:
Be sure the adjective clause is placed next to the word it modifies.

Hint 4:
See Chapter 9, Rule 4 for punctuation of nonrestrictive adjective clauses.

PART III: ADVERB CLAUSE

A. Characteristics:

1. The adverb clause will have a subject and a verb and will start with one of these words:

after	because	though
although	before	unless
as	even though	until
as if	if	when
as long as	in order that	whenever
as much as	provided that	where
as soon as	since	wherever
as though	so that	while
	than	

2. Other characteristics of the adverb clause are similar to those of noun clauses.

B. Function:
The adverb clause functions just as a single-word adverb: it modifies verbs, adjectives, and other adverbs; and it tells *when, where, why, how, to what extent,* and *under what conditions.*

The following examples, using each of the special introductory words listed above, show how adverb clauses function.

Example 1:
After he washed the car, the sky clouded, threatening rain.
(Subject, *he;* verb, *washed;* tells *when* about the verb *clouded.*)

Example 2:
Although the water was choppy, we found skiing conditions excellent.
(Subject, *water;* verb, *was;* tells *under what conditions* about the verb *found.*)

Example 3:
The shoppers dashed inside *as the rain began.*
(Subject, *rain;* verb, *began;* tells *when* about the verb *dashed.*)

Example 4:
The puppy ate *as if he had been without food for days.*
(Subject, *he;* verb, *had been;* tells *how* about the verb *ate.*)

Example 5:
He spent money *as long as he had it.*
Subject, *he;* verb, *had;* tells *when* about the verb *spent.*)

Example 6:
I worked *as much as he did.*
(Subject, *he;* verb, *did;* tells *to what extent* about the verb *worked.*)

Example 7:
As soon as we could, we donned swim suits and headed for the pool.
(Subject, *we;* verb, *could;* tells *when* about the verb *donned.*)

Example 8:
He studied *as though his life depended upon it.*
(Subject, *life;* verb, *depended;* tells *how* or *to what extent* about the verb *studied.*)

Example 9:
Because the flood waters receded slowly, deep layers of mud were left behind.
(Subject, *waters;* verb, *receded;* tells *why* about the verb *were left.*)

Example 10:
Aunt Thelma left *before we could say goodbye.*
(Subject, *we;* verb, *could say;* tells *when* about the verb *left.*)

Example 11:
I was angry *even though I understood his error.*
(Subject, *I;* verb, *understood;* tells *under what conditions* about the predicate adjective *angry.*)

Example 12:
If you fail to pay your taxes, you will be penalized.
(Subject, *you;* verb, *fail;* tells *under what conditions* about the verb *will be penalized.*)

Example 13:
In order that yesterday's filing would be completed, Jane worked two hours' overtime.
(Subject, *filing;* verb, *would be completed;* tells *why* about the verb *worked.*)

Example 14:
The desk would fit in the room, *provided that it was pushed snugly against the wall.*
(Subject, *it;* verb, *was pushed;* tells *under what conditions* about the verb *would fit.*)

Example 15:
Since yesterday's snow storm ended, we felt little security in camping out for the remainder of the week.
(Subject, *storm;* verb, *ended;* tells *when* about the verb *felt.*)

Example 16:
Juan rewrote his paper *so that it would be letter perfect.*
(Subject, *it;* verb, *would be;* tells *why* about the verb *rewrote.*)

Example 17:
Martin worked harder *than Bill did.*
(Subject, Bill; verb, *did;* tells *to what extent* about the adverb *harder.*)

Example 18:
Though mosquitoes swarmed above us, they did not attack us until after dark.
(Subject, *mosquitoes;* verb, *swarmed;* tells *under what conditions* about the verb *did attack.*)

Example 19:
Unless we collapse from exhaustion first, we plan to finish cleaning the fish within an hour.
(Subject, *we;* verb, *collapse;* tells *under what conditions* about the verb *plan.*)

Example 20:
When I attend a wedding, I almost always cry.
(Subject, *I;* verb, *attend;* tells *when* about the verb *cry.*)

Example 21:
Our dog barks and growls *whenever the meter-reader comes into the yard.*
(Subject, *reader;* verb, *comes;* tells *when* about the compound verb *barks and growls.*)

Example 22:
While the flagman dozed in the afternoon sun, his assistant directed traffic.
(Subject, *flagman;* verb, *dozed;* tells *when* about the verb *directed.*)

Warning A:
Some adverb clauses have a missing—but implied—verb.

> *Example:*
> The assistant instructor worked harder preparing for the class *than I.*
> (Adverb clause: *than I* [did])

Warning B:
Some adverb clauses have a missing—but implied—subject.

Example 1:
While driving to St. Louis, he decided to travel on roads other than interstate highways.
(Adverb clause: *while* [he was] *driving to St. Louis*)

Example 2:
When putting up a tent, she always gets tangled in the ropes.
(Adverb clause: *when* [she is] *putting up a tent*)

Hint:
Be sure that you do not say something ridiculous—even unintentionally—when there are implied subjects.

Example:

Ridiculous: When putting up a tent, the ropes often get in the way. (Since the subject is implied, the reader may think you intend *ropes* to be the subject! Ropes are not very good at putting up tents!)

Improved: When putting up a tent, you must keep the ropes untangled.
(Adverb clause: *when* [you are] *putting up a tent*)

Warning C:
Do not confuse adverb clauses with prepositional phrases.

Example 1:
After dinner, I took a nap.
(*After* plus the noun *dinner* makes a prepositional phrase.)

Compare that with the following:

Example 2:
After we ate dinner, I took a nap.
(*After* and a subject and a verb make an adverb clause.)

Example 3:
I have slept *since one o'clock.*
(*Since* and a noun make a prepositional phrase.)

Compare that with the following:

Example 4:
I have slept *since I came home from work.*
(*Since* and a subject and verb make an adverb clause.)

Remember:
A clause must have a subject and a verb. A phrase does not.

Hint:
See Chapter 9, Rule 5 for punctuation of adverb clauses.

REVIEW

Work through the following sentences to find all the noun, adjective, and adverb clauses. Identify the function of each clause. Answers are printed after the sentences, but see if you really understand these clauses before you check. And read carefully. Many sentences have more than one subordinate clause!

Sentences

1. His new car, which was a four-cylinder model, gave him good gas mileage.

2. After the airplane engine was overhauled, the mechanic who had done most of the work pronounced the engine in good shape.

3. Honey bees, industrious creatures that they are, usually work themselves to death after six weeks of gathering honey.

4. Because the July heat was oppressive, the two hikers rested whenever they had the opportunity.

5. Whoever discovered that cooking dried corn in lye water makes hominy aided dietetic variety.

6. The dulcimer, which makes mandolin-like music, is not readily available in most music stores.

7. Because rip-rap rock is quite large, whoever works with it will be exhausted after he handles the first ton or so.

8. Whichever tree limbs are to be pruned should be clearly marked so that no one cuts off the wrong ones.

9. Whoever owns those Chinese geese that make such raucous noises must not be able to hear them when they create such a commotion that it awakens the entire neighborhood.

10. As the wind freshened, we anticipated a storm.

Solutions

1. *Which was a four-cylinder model* is an adjective clause that tells *which* about the noun *car*.

2. *After the airplane engine was overhauled* is an adverb clause that tells *when* about the verb *pronounced. Who had done most of the work* is an adjective clause that tells *which* about the noun *mechanic*.

3. *That they are* is an adjective clause that tells *what kind* about the noun *creatures. After* begins a prepositional phrase, not an adverb clause.

4. *Because the July heat was oppressive* is an adverb clause that tells *why* about the verb *rested. Whenever they had the opportunity* is an adverb clause that tells *when* about the verb *rested.*

5. *Whoever discovered that cooking dried corn in lye water makes hominy* is a noun clause that is the subject of the sentence. *That cooking dried corn in lye water makes hominy* is also a noun clause that is the object of the verb *discovered.* (So you have a clause within a clause. Fancy!)

6. *Which makes mandolin-like music* is an adjective clause that tells *what kind* about the noun *dulcimer.*

7. *Because rip-rap rock is quite large* is an adverb clause that tells *why* about the verb *will be exhausted. Whoever works with it* is a noun clause that is the subject of the main verb *will be exhausted. After he handles the first ton or so* is an adverb clause that tells *when* about the verb *will be exhausted.* (Did you find all three?)

8. *Whichever tree limbs are to be pruned* is a noun clause that is the subject of the sentence. *So that no one cuts off the wrong ones* is an adverb clause that tells *why* about the verb *should be marked.*

9. *Whoever owns those Chinese geese that make such raucous noises* is a noun clause that is subject of the sentence. *That make such raucous noises* is an adjective clause that tells *which* about the noun *geese.* (So you have a clause within a clause again!) *When they create such a commotion that it awakens the entire neighborhood* is an adverb clause that tells *when* about the infinitive *to hear. That it awakens the entire neighborhood* is an adjective clause within the adverb clause that tells *what kind* about the noun *commotion.* (All three kinds of clauses in one sentence!)

10. *As the wind freshened* is an adverb clause that tells *when* about the verb *anticipated.*

IV

PUNCTUATION

9

COMMAS

Now that you have a command of the fundamentals of grammar and the basic principles of usage, you are ready to punctuate. In an effort to simplify the many rules for using commas, this chapter condenses the rules to seven. These seven rules will solve ninety-nine percent of your problems.

Remember:

If there is no rule to indicate the need for a comma, do not use one. It is just as wrong to use unnecessary commas as it is to leave them out.

RULES

Rule 1: Use a comma to separate items in a series. A series is made up of three or more items. A series can be made up of nouns, verbs, modifiers, or phrases.

Examples:

—Series of *nouns: Dogs,* trapeze *artists,* and *clowns* all tumbled down the aisle together.

—Series of *verbs:* The old truck *coughed, lurched,* and then *shuddered.*

—Series of *modifiers:* Those hamburgers were *greasy, tasteless,* and *too small.*

—Series of *phrases:* We looked *under the rug, behind the pictures,* but not *inside the cabinet.*

Hint A:
To be safe and to avoid possible confusion, include the comma before the joining words like and, or, or nor: A, B, and C.

Example:
John, Tom, and Sue inherited $15,000.

Hint B:
If each item has a joining word after it, use no commas: A and B and C; A or B or C.

Example 1:
We swam and ate and slept for five days.

Example 2:
Milk or water or even ink would have tasted good to us.

Hint C:
Use no comma after the last item.

Example:
Maple, oak, and walnut trees provided dense shade.

Rule 2: Use a comma to separate coordinate adjectives. Coordinate adjectives are two or more adjectives that equally modify the same noun.

Example:
The low, heavy clouds threatened snow.
(*Low* and *heavy* both modify *clouds.*)

To Test:
You must be able to substitute *and* for the comma separating coordinate adjectives. Otherwise, you will use no comma.

Example 1:
A sleek, shiny new car sat in the driveway.
A sleek [and] shiny new car sat in the driveway.
But not: A sleek [and] shiny [and] new car sat in the driveway.

Example 2:
That pink flowering tree is especially pretty in the spring.
(*Pink* modifies *flowering* and *flowering* modifies *tree.* No comma. We cannot say, *that pink and flowering tree.*)

Warning A:
Use no comma if the word *and, or,* or *nor* actually appears between the two adjectives.

Example:
The long and arduous journey left the explorer with many memories, both pleasant and unpleasant.

Warning B:
Omit the comma before *numbers* and before adjectives of *size, shape,* and *age.*

Example 1:
Three tired hikers napped against the tree trunks.
(No comma after *three;* it is a *number.*)

Example 2:
The huge old house stood alone on the hill.
(No comma after *huge;* it is an adjective of *size.* And *old* is also an adjective of *age.*)

Example 3:
A dilapidated two-storied house stood next door.
(No comma after *dilapidated* since *two-storied* is an adjective of *shape.*)

Rule 3: Use a comma to separate two complete sentences joined by a conjunction (*and, but, or, nor,* or *for,* and sometimes *yet* and *so*).

Example 1:
Joan walked to the shopping center, but she found the stores all closed.
(You will see that we have joined two sentences with the conjunction *but: Joan walked to the shopping center. She found the stores all closed.* As you join the two sentences with *but,* replace the period with a comma so that you put the comma at the end of the first sentence.)

Compare that example with this one:

Example 2:
Joan walked to the shopping center and found that the stores were closed.
(Notice that you need *no* comma here since there are not two complete sentences—the verb is merely compound.)

Remember:
With this rule, think of a comma plus a conjunction like *and, but, or, nor,* or *for* as being equal to a period. If you could not put in a period instead of the comma and conjunction, you do not have two sentences. Think of the rule this way:

$$, + \left\{ \begin{array}{l} and \\ but \\ or \\ nor \\ for \end{array} \right\} = .$$

Warning:
Be sure you have a complete sentence both before *and* after the conjunctions *and, but, or, nor,* or *for* before you put in a comma. Try substituting the period for the *comma and conjunction* to see if you have two sentences:

Example 1:
The calculator needed new batteries, but it seemed to be functioning accurately.

Two complete sentences:
—The calculator needed new batteries.
—It seemed to be functioning accurately.

(Two complete sentences are joined with a comma and a conjunction.)

Example 2:
The calculator needed new batteries but seemed to be functioning accurately.

One complete sentence:
—The calculator needed new batteries.
— . . . seemed to be functioning accurately.

(Since the second group of words is not a sentence, we do *not* use a comma and conjunction. We could *not* substitute with a period.)

Rule 4: Set off nonrestrictive verbal phrases or adjective clauses with commas.

A. *Set off* implies *two* commas—one before and one after—unless the phrase or clause is at the end of the sentence.

B. *Nonrestrictive* means "not essential" or "not needed to limit the noun."

C. A verbal phrase is a word group that begins with an infinitive or participle (see Chapter 7).

D. An adjective clause is a word group that has a subject and verb and starts with *who, whose, whom, which,* or *that* (see Chapter 8, Part II, Adjective Clauses).

Example 1:
The brick house that was built across the street is for sale, but the brick house that was built next door is already sold.
(The adjective clauses *that was built across the street* and *that was built next door* are restrictive; that is, they are *necessary* to limit the noun they modify: *house.* Notice that if we read the sentence without the clauses, the sentence would not make much sense: The brick house is for sale, but the brick house is already sold.)

Example 2:
My sporty red Fiat, which my father gave me, is no longer in operating condition.
(The clause *which my father gave me* is not needed to limit *my sporty red Fiat.* I have only one! So the information in the clause is added information.)

Hint:
Think of added information as being a "by the way" idea: By the way, my father gave me the Fiat. *By setting that information off with commas, you are saying that the "by the way" idea can be dropped out:*

> My sporty red Fiat)
> which [*by the way*] my father gave me)
> is no longer in operating condition.
> (Think of the commas as arrows showing that the idea can be dropped without affecting the meaning of the noun it modifies, *Fiat.*)

Example 3:
Mr. Tzachosky, just getting off the boat, is a military agent.
(*Just getting off the boat* is a nonrestrictive—that is, nonessential—participial phrase. It is not needed to limit all Mr. Tzachoskys to just one. There is just one about whom the reader knows. The commas indicate that *just getting off the boat* is "by the way" information that can be dropped out.)

Rule 5: Set off introductory elements with a comma. Obviously, introductory elements appear at the beginning of the sentence! There are three kinds of introductory elements:

A. Introductory single words

Examples:
Yes, I'm going to the game.

Oh, did you mean that?

Kathy, please open the door.

B.   Introductory prepositional phrases of four or more words

Example 1:
Behind the door of the closet, we found the kitten asleep.
(Use the comma after this prepositional phrase. It has six words.)

Example 2:
Around the corner we ran into old friends.
(No comma is necessary after a prepositional phrase of only three words.)

C.   Introductory verbal modifiers (see Chapter 7)

Example 1:
Walking home from work, he spotted two new species of birds in the neighborhood.
(Introductory participial phrase modifying *he*)

Example 2:
To catch an early bus, he left home fifteen minutes ahead of schedule.
(Introductory infinitive phrase modifying *he*)

Warning:
If you use a comma, be sure the verbal is a *modifier,* not a subject.

   Example 1:
   Walking home from work is his usual form of exercise.
   (Use no comma after *work* since *walking home from work* is the subject of the sentence.)

   Example 2:
   To catch an early bus was his daily goal.
   (Use no comma after *bus* since *to catch an early bus* is the subject of the sentence.)

D.   Introductory adverb clause (see Chapter 8, Part III, Adverb Clauses)

Example 1:
After we left, the rain began.
(Subject, *we;* verb, *left;* tells *when* about *began.*)

Example 2:
Because we all had eaten too much, most of us fell asleep.
(Subject, *we;* verb, *had eaten;* tells *why* about *fell.*)

Example 3:
If you know the answer, don't tell!
(Subject, *you;* verb, *know;* tells *under what condition* about *tell.*)

Note:
Unlike the limit of four words before using a comma after the introductory prepositional phrase (see Rule 5), there is no limit regarding adverb clauses.

Example:
If you can, call me about noon.
(Comma after only three words; it is an introductory adverb clause!)

Rule 6: Use commas to set off interrupters. Interrupters come in the middle of the sentence and interrupt its natural flow. There are three kinds of interrupters.

A. Appositives (An appositive is a noun with its modifiers that re-names another noun.)

Example:
Thornton Kleug, *a local author of some acclaim,* spoke at the Elks meeting.
(*A local author of some acclaim* is a noun, along with modifiers, that renames *Thornton Kleug.*)

Note:
When an appositive appears at the end of the sentence, you will, of course, have only one comma.

B. Words of direct address (*Direct address* refers to speaking directly to someone.)

Example 1:
Will you, *John,* please close the door.

Example 2:
May I, *friends and neighbors,* ask your support?

Hint:
Compare these examples with Rule 5, Part A. If the noun of direct address comes at the beginning, you may think of it as introductory (requiring only one comma). If the noun of direct address comes in the middle of the sentence—interrupts the sentence— then you need a comma both before and after to set it off. If the noun of direct address comes at the end of the sentence, you will have only one comma.

C. Parenthetical expressions
The following are typical—but not all—parenthetical expressions:

of course	*in fact*	*moreover*
in the meantime	*I believe*	*consequently*
on the other hand	*I hope*	*for example*
therefore	*I think*	*nevertheless*
however	*indeed*	*he said*

Example 1:
Our texbooks, *on the other hand,* are more thorough than the workbooks.

Example 2:
That so-called breeze, *as a matter of fact,* is more like a gale.

Example 3:
"We will," John said, "complete the work as planned."

Note:
Dozens of other interrupting phrases like *he explained, he yelled, he whispered* are set off by commas when they interrupt, precede, or follow direct quotations. See Chapter 11, Part IV for a discussion of direct quotations.

Warning:
Sometimes these parenthetical expressions are used to join two sentences together. Then commas are not sufficient. See Chapter 10.

Rule 7: Use commas to set off dates and states.

Example 1:
Date:	January 5, 1935
Month and year:	January 1935 (no comma needed)
Sentence:	January 5, 1935, was the date of her birth. (two commas needed)

Example 2:
City and state:	Louisville, Kentucky
Sentence:	Louisville, Kentucky, is her home. (two commas needed)

Summary for Using Commas

Rule 1: Series

Rule 2: Coordinate adjectives
(except size, shape, age, and numbers)

Rule 3: Two sentences with conjunction
_____, and _____.

Rule 4: Nonrestrictive
    A. Adjective clause
    B. Verbal phrase

Rule 5: Introductory
    A. Single words
    B. Prepositional phrase of four or more words
    C. Verbal modifier
    D. Adverb clause

Rule 6: Interrupters
    A. Appositive
    B. Direct address
    C. Parenthetical expressions

Rule 7: Dates and states

There is a complete review of punctuation at the end of Chapter 11.

10

SEMICOLONS AND COLONS

In a continuing effort to make punctuation as plain and simple as possible, this chapter gives three rules for using semicolons and three rules for using colons.

PART I: SEMICOLONS

There are three basic reasons for using semicolons:

A. Use a semicolon to join two sentences when there is *no* coordinating conjunction like *and, but, or, nor, for,* and sometimes *yet* and *so.*
    Think of this diagram to help you remember:

    _____(sentence)_____ , *and* _____(sentence)_____.
    OR
    _____(sentence)_____ ; _____(sentence)_____.

Example:
Sue Ellen missed the bus, *so* she was late to school.
Sue Ellen missed the bus; she was late to school.

Warning:
When sentences are joined by a conjunctive adverb, such as *consequently, therefore, nevertheless, moreover, however,* you need not only a semicolon *before* but a comma *after* the conjunctive adverb. (See Rule 6 in Chapter 9.)

Example:
Sue Ellen missed the bus; *therefore,* she was late to school.

Think of these diagrams when joining two sentences:

_____(sentence)_____ , *and* _____(sentence)_____.
_____(sentence)_____ ; _____(sentence)_____.
_____(sentence)_____ ; *therefore,* _____(sentence)_____.

Hint:
To be joined with a semicolon, the ideas in the two sentences should be closely related.

Example:
George and his father fished steadily for six hours; their efforts were futile.

B.　Use a semicolon to separate two sentences that are joined by a conjunction but that have other commas within either of the two sentences.

Think of the following diagram to clarify the rule:
(Each line represents a complete sentence.)

    _____ , *and* _____ .
    _____,_____ ; *and* _____ .
    _____ ; *and* _____,_____ .
    _____,_____ ; *and* _____,_____ .

Example:
The teachers were eager to go home, *but* they took with them all the papers to be graded for the next week.
(The comma and conjunction *but* are sufficient to separate the two sentences.)

When school was dismissed Friday, the teachers were eager to go home; *but* they took with them all the papers to be graded for the next week.
(Now we have a comma in the first sentence—an introductory element, Rule 5—so the comma and conjunction *but* are no longer sufficient. The comma in front of *but* becomes a semicolon.)

C.　Use a semicolon to separate items in a series if there are commas within the items.

Example 1:
Mr. Brown had baked a cake; Miss Johnson, an apple pie; Mrs. Rolfe, a pan of biscuits.
(There are three items in the series:
　　1.　Mr. Brown had baked a cake
　　2.　Miss Johnson, an apple pie
　　3.　Mrs. Rolfe, a pan of biscuits
Since there are commas within the items themselves, the items must be separated from each other with *semicolons.*)

Example 2:
The prize winners came from Waukegan. Illinois; Denton, Texas; and Hillside, New York.
(The three items in the series are as follows:
　　1.　Waukegan, Illinois
　　2.　Denton, Texas
　　3.　Hillside, New York
Since there are commas within the items, the items must be separated with semicolons.)

PART II: COLONS

There are three reasons for using a colon:

A. Use a colon for certain conventional items.

    1. Giving the time

    Example:
    3:15 PM

    2. Separating chapter from verse in Bible references

    Example:
    John 3:16

    3. Separating volume from page in bibliography references

    Example:
    Reader's Digest 146:72
    (The volume is 146 and the page is 72.)

    4. Giving a salutation in a business letter

    Example:
    Dear Sir:

B. Use a colon to introduce a formal list.

Example:
We bought the following items: ground beef, hamburger buns, potato chips, and cokes.

Hint:
The words following *or* as follows *or* these *are often clue words.*

Warning:
Do *not* use a colon after a preposition or after a linking verb.

Remember:
Prepositions are followed by objects, and linking verbs are followed by predicate words. Sometimes, these objects and predicate words are compound, or even in a series. But *do not* separate the preposition from its object or the linking verb from its predicate word with *any* kind of punctuation.

    Example 1:
    The days for make-up exams are Tuesday, Wednesday, and Thursday.
    (Do not use a colon after the linking verb *are.*)

    Example 2:
    The days for make-up exams are the following: Tuesday, Wednesday, and Thursday.
    (Use a colon after the clue word *following* to introduce a list.)

Example 3:
Make-up exams will be given on these dates: June 6, 7, and 8.
(Use a colon after the clue word *these* to introduce a list.)

Hint:
Sometimes a complete thought can end in a preposition or linking verb. In that case—and only in that case—a colon can follow a preposition or linking verb.

Example 1:
I know what the answers are: A, B, B, A.
(A complete thought precedes the linking verb.)

Example 2:
I know what it is made of: rubber and wood.
(A complete thought precedes the preposition.)

The reason for these colons in the two above examples is explained in the following rule:

C. Use a colon to mean "summary follows" or "explanation follows." The explanation is usually a complete sentence, and the summary is usually a series of words or phrases.

Example 1:
He was limping badly: he had burned his foot when he spilled the boiling water.
(The second sentence explains the first.)

Example 2:
The theater boasted a successful season: excellent ticket sales, increased revenue, stable expenditures, and favorable critics' reviews.
(The items after the colon summarize the conditions involved in a successful season.)

Summary for Using Semicolons and Colons

I. **Semicolons**

  A. Joining sentences with no conjunction
    _____ ; _____ .
    _____ ; *therefore,* _____ .

  B. Separating two sentences with conjunction and other commas
    _____ , _____; *and* _____.
    _____; *and* _____ , _____.
    _____ , _____; *and* _____ , _____.

  C. Separating items in a series if commas appear within the items

II. **Colons**

  A. Conventional items

B. List
    (except after prepositions or linking verbs)

C. "Summary or explanation follows"

There is a complete review of punctuation at the end of Chapter 11.

11

OTHER PUNCTUATION

Since most other marks of punctuation are relatively simple, only the bare minimum is included here.

PART I: END MARKS

A. **Period**

1. Use a period at the end of a statement.

2. Use a period for an abbreviation.

    Hint:
    Most governmental agency and international organization abbreviations are not followed with periods.

    Examples:
    Interstate Commerce Commission = ICC
    United Nations = UN

B. **Exclamation Point**

Use an exclamation point at the end of an exclamatory sentence or expression.

Example:
What a game*!*

C. **Question Mark**

1. Use a question mark to ask a question.

    Example:
    Where is the nearest gas station*?*

2. Do not use a question mark after an indirect question.

    Example:
    I wonder where the nearest gas station is.

3. It is not usually necessary to use a question mark after a polite command.

    Example:
    Mary, will you please come here.

PART II: APOSTROPHES

A. Use the apostrophe to show possession.

   1. Use the following steps to formulate the possessive:

      a. Write the word to be made possessive in a prepositional phrase.

         Example 1:
         That *cats* ears are pointed.
         The ears *of that cat* are pointed.

         Example 2:
         All the team *members* shoes are wet.
         The shoes *of all the team members* are wet.

         Example 3:
         He earned two *weeks* pay.
         He earned the pay *of two weeks.*

         Example 4:
         An *hours* time is all I can spare.
         The time *of an hour* is all I can spare.

      b. Add the apostrophe to the object of the preposition and eliminate the other words.

         Examples:

         . . .cat'

         . . .members'

         . . .weeks'

         . . .hour'

      c. If the word does not end in an -*s*, add it.

         Examples:

cat'	cat's	—The *cat's* ears are pointed.
members'	(no change)	—All the team *members'* shoes are wet.
weeks'	(no change)	—He earned two *weeks'* pay.
hour'	hour's	—An *hour's* time is all I can spare.

   2. Some peculiar situations sometimes result when forming possessives:

      a. If you add an apostrophe to a *singular* word that ends in -*s* and that is just one syllable, then you *will* add another -*s*.

         Examples:

         —Charles's
         (*Charles* is singular and only one syllable, so you need the extra -*s*.)

—waitress'
(*Waitress* is singular but two syllables, so you do *not* add an extra *-s*.)

    b. Compound words are usually made plural at the end of the first word and always made possessive at the end of the second:

Examples:

sister-in-law

two sisters-in-law (plural)

sister-in-law's car (possessive)

two sisters-in-law's cars (plural possessive)

    c. Sometimes two people are involved in ownership.

        1) If two people own something together, the second word shows the ownership.

Example:
Mother and Dad's house
(jointly owned)

        2) If two people own something separately, *both* words show ownership.

Example:
Eisenhower's and Kennedy's administrations
(Each had his own administration.)

B. Use apostrophes to show omissions.

Examples:

cannot–can't

crash of 1929—crash of '29

C. Use apostrophes to show plurals of letters, signs, numbers, and words referred to as words.

Examples:

Avoid *you*'s in formal writing.   See also Part III,

Be sure to cross your *t*'s   Italics, Section C

PART III: ITALICS

(Italics are made in handwritten work by underlining.)

A. Use italics for foreign words.

Example:
He graduated *summa cum laude.*

B.   Use italics for titles of long works like books, periodicals, and movies. (Compare with Part IV, Quotation Marks, Section B.)

Example:
The latest issue of *US News and World Report* is lying on the sofa.

C.   Use italics for letters or words referred to as such.

Examples:
The *i* looked like an *e.*
Too many *and*'s appeared in the paragraph.
(See also Part II, Apostrophes, Section C.)

PART IV: QUOTATION MARKS

A.   Use quotation marks to set off someone's direct words.

Example 1:
He said, "I watched the moon rise late last night."
(His exact words are in quotation marks.)

Example 2:
He said that he watched the moon rise late last night.
(No quotation marks needed. His direct words are not given.)

B.   Use quotation marks around titles of smaller works.

Example:
"How to Retire Early" appeared in last month's issue of *Business Week.*

Compare this rule with Part III, Italics, Section B. Then, think in terms of the following summary:

Italics	*Quotation Marks*
name of magazine	magazine article
name of book	chapter in book
name of newspaper	newspaper article
name of musical	individual song

C.   Use quotation marks around the definition of a word.

Example:
Austere means "serious, stern."
(Compare with Part III, Italics, Section C. The word *austere* is italicized since it is referred to as a word, but the definition of that word goes in quotation marks.)

PLACEMENT OF MULTIPLE PUNCTUATION MARKS

Now let us consider some general rules for the placement of punctuation marks when more than one mark is needed after a single word.

Rule 1: Never use two end marks of punctuation together.

Rule 2: Never use a comma with an end mark.

Rule 3: When using quotation marks,
         —put periods and commas *inside* closing quotation marks.

         Examples:
         ."

         ,"

         Not ",

              ".

         —put question marks and exclamation marks either inside or outside
           closing quotation marks, depending on which part of the sentence is
           the question or exclamation.

Example 1:
The skier asked, "Is the chair lift operating yet?"
(The question mark goes with the question *Is the chair lift operating yet.*)

Example 2:
Did the skier say, "I'm planning to ski the west slope"?
(The whole sentence, not the quotation, is the question. The question
mark goes *after* the quotation marks.)

         —put semicolons and colons outside closing quotation marks.

Example:
The man threatened, "I won't help you"; however, I didn't believe him.

REVIEW

You now have the basics of punctuation! Using the summaries at the ends of Chapters 9 and 10 to refresh your memory, apply what you have learned in these last three chapters to complete the following punctuation review. When you have punctuated these sentences as accurately as you can, check your answers with those that follow the sentences. Rule and section numbers are given with the answers so that you can review those items which may still be causing you some difficulty.

Sentences

1. After we watched the martins diving acrobatics for nearly an hour Delbert the local ornithologist explained how they feed on insects caught in midair.

2. The following pear trees were grouped together in the orchard Bartlett Golden Delicious and his favorite Starking Delicious.

3. Gentlemen may I ask your support in Barbara and Gerald endeavor in working with The Daily News he said.

4. My editor-in-chief attitude which was indeed not at all difficult to accept reflected his superior education and extensive experience.

5. Changing flat tires adjusting carburetors and checking the timing were part of his daily work but he resented doing that same work at home for nonpaying relatives.

6. Yes many people believe that Boonville Indiana located in the southern tip of the state was named after Daniel Boone.

7. Ruffled by the wind the tall golden wheat makes a cool and restful summer scene except to the farmer who finds harvesting the wheat and baling the straw hot itchy work.

8. The elevated highway described in the pamphlet Getting Around Town provided quick transportation around the city but gaining access to it was a real puzzle.

9. In the left-hand corner of the top drawer you will find my dear a special surprise package for you.

10. Studying horoscopes interests her for a special reason she believes her own life is guided by the sign of Capricorn.

11. Talking in front of his peers gave him practice talking in front of strangers became easier.

12. Those committee members who worked most diligently at this assignment will be financially rewarded and recognized at the national meeting.

Solutions

1. After we watched the martins' diving acrobatics for nearly an hour, Delbert, the local ornithologist, explained how they feed on insects caught in midair.

martins' (Chapter 11, Part II, Section A)
hour, (Chapter 9, Rule 5, Part D)
Delbert, ornithologist, (Chapter 9, Rule 6, Part A)

2. The following pear trees were grouped together in the orchard: Bartlett;
   Golden Delicious; and his favorite, Starking Delicious.
   orchard: (Chapter 10, Part II, Section B or C)
   Bartlett; (Chapter 10, Part I, Section C)
   Delicious; (Chapter 10, Part I, Section C)
   favorite, (Chapter 9, Rule 6, Part A)

3. "Gentlemen, may I ask your support in Barbara and Gerald's endeavor in
   working with *The Daily News*," he said.
   "Gentlemen (Chapter 11, Part IV, Section A)
   Gentlemen, (Chapter 9, Rule 5, Part A)
   Barbara and Gerald's (Chapter 11, Part II, Section A, 2, c)
   The Daily News (Chapter 11, Part III, Section B)
   News, (Chapter 9, Rule 6, Part C. Note: a question mark is not necessary
   as internal punctuation because this is a polite request, not a question.)
   News," (Chapter 11, Part IV, Section A)

4. My editor-in-chief's attitude, which was, indeed, not at all difficult to accept,
   reflected his superior education and extensive experience.
   editor-in-chief's (Chapter 11, Part II, Section A, 2, b)
   attitude, (Chapter 9, Rule 4, Part A)
   was, indeed, (Chapter 9, Rule 6, Part C)
   accept, (Chapter 9, Rule 4, Part A)

5. Changing flat tires, adjusting carburetors, and checking the timing were part
   of his daily work; but he resented doing that same work at home for nonpaying relatives.
   tires, carburetors, (Chapter 9, Rule 1)
   work; (Chapter 10, Part I, Section B)

6. Yes, many people believe that Boonville, Indiana, located in the southern tip
   of the state, was named after Daniel Boone.
   Yes, (Chapter 9, Rule 5, Part A)
   Boonville, (Chapter 9, Rule 7)
   Indiana, (Chapter 9, Rule 7 or Rule 4, Part B)
   state, (Chapter 9, Rule 4, Part B)

7. Ruffled by the wind, the tall, golden wheat makes a cool and restful summer
   scene except to the farmer, who finds harvesting the wheat and baling the
   straw hot, itchy work.
   wind, (Chapter 9, Rule 5, Part C)
   tall, (Chapter 9, Rule 2)
   farmer, (Chapter 9, Rule 4, Part A)
   hot, (Chapter 9, Rule 2)

8. The elevated highway described in the pamphlet "Getting Around Town"
   provided quick transportation around the city, but gaining access to it was a
   real puzzle.
   "Getting Around Town" (Chapter 11, Part IV, Section B)
   city, (Chapter 9, Rule 3)

left-hand corner of the top drawer, you will find, my dear, a special surprise package for you.
drawer, (Chapter 9, Rule 5, Part B)
find, dear, (Chapter 9, Rule 6, Part B)

10. Studying horoscopes interests her for a special reason: she believes her own life is guided by the sign of Capricorn.
reason: (Chapter 10, Part II, Section C)

11. Talking in front of his peers gave him practice; talking in front of strangers became easier.
practice; (Chapter 10, Part I, Section A)

12. No further punctuation needed